The
Phenomenon™

The
Phenomenon™

Achieve More in the
Next 12 Months
Than the
Previous 12 Years

Dan Kennedy
and 26 Practitioners of The Phenomenon™

A PART OF ADVANTAGE MEDIA GROUP

Published by Elevate, Charleston, South Carolina.
Member of Advantage Media Group.

ELEVATE is a registered trademark and the Elevate colophon is a trademark of Advantage Media Group, Inc.

This publication is designed to provide accurate and authoritative information in regard to the subject matter covered. It is sold with the understanding that the publisher is not engaged in rendering legal, accounting, or other professional services. If legal advice or other expert assistance is required, the services of a competent professional person should be sought. No income claims or representations are being made by the publishers and authors.

Printed in the United States of America.

ISBN: 978-1-60194-031-5

Most Advantage Media Group titles are available at special quantity discounts for bulk purchases for sales promotions, premiums, fundraising, and educational use. Special versions or book excerpts can also be created to fit specific needs.

For more information, please write: Special Markets, Advantage Media Group, P.O. Box 272, Charleston, SC 29402 or call 1.866.775.1696.

Visit us online at **advantagefamily**.com

Table of Contents

Special Opportunity for Readers of "The PHENOMENON™"...

The Most Incredible
<u>FREE</u> Gift Ever

($613.91 Worth of Pure MoneyMaking Information)

Dan Kennedy & Bill Glazer are offering an incredible opportunity for you to see WHY <u>Glazer-Kennedy Insider's Circle</u>™ is known as "THE PLACE" where entrepreneurs seeking FAST and Dramatic Growth and greater Control, Independence, and Security come together. Dan & Bill want to give you **$613.91 worth of pure Money-Making Information** including TWO months as an 'Elite' Gold Member of Glazer-Kennedy's Insider's Circle™. You'll receive a steady stream of MILLIONAIRE Maker Information including:

★ **Glazer-Kennedy University: Series of 3 Webinars (Value = $387.00)**

The 10 "BIG Breakthroughs in Business Life *with Dan Kennedy*

- HOW <u>Any</u> Entrepreneur or Sales Professional can Multiply INCOME by 10X
- **HOW to Avoid Once and for All being an *"Advertising Victim"***
- The "*Hidden Goldmine*" in Everyone's Business and HOW to Capitalize on it
- **The BIGGEST MISTAKE most Entrepreneurs make in their Marketing**
- And the <u>BIGGEEE</u>...Getting Customers Seeking You Out.

The ESSENTIALS to Writing Million Dollar Ads & Sales Letters BOTH Online & Offline *with Bill Glazer*

- How to INCREASE the Selling Power of <u>All</u> Your Advertising with the 13 "Must Have" Direct Response Principles
- **Key Elements that Determine the Success of Your Website**
- How to Craft a Headline the Grabs the Reader's Attention
- **HOW to Create an Irresistible Offer that Melts Away <u>Any</u> Resistance to Buy**
- The <u>Best</u> Ways to Create Urgency and Inspire IMMEDIATE Response
- "*Insider Strategies*" to INCREASE Response you <u>Must</u> be using both ONLINE & Offline

The ESSENTIALS of Productivity & Implementation for Entrepreneurs *with Peak Performance Coach Lee Milteer*

- How to Almost INSTANTLY be MORE Effective, Creative, and Profitable
- **HOW to Master the "Inner Game" of Personal Peak Productivity**
- How to Get MORE Done in Less Time and Take MORE Time Off
- **HOW to Get Others to Work On <u>Your</u> Schedule**
- How to Create Clear Goals for SUCESSFUL Implementation
- **And Finally the <u>BIGGEE</u>...HOW to Stop Talking and Planning Your Dreams and Start Implementing them into Reality**

★ **'Elite' Gold Insider's Circle Membership (Two Month Value = $99.94):**

● TWO Issues of *The NO B.S. Marketing Letter:*

Each issue is at least 12 pages – usually MORE – Overflowing with **the latest Marketing & MoneyMaking Strategies**. Current members refer to it as <u>a day-long intense seminar in print</u>, arriving by first class mail every month. There are ALWAYS terrific examples of *"What's-Working-NOW"* **Strategies**, timely Marketing news, trends, ongoing teaching of <u>Dan Kennedy's Most IMPORTANT Strategies</u>... and MORE. As soon as it arrives in your mailbox you'll want to find a quiet place, grab a highlighter, and devour every word.

- TWO CDs Of The **EXCLUSIVE GOLD AUDIO INTERVIEWS**

  These are EXCLUSIVE interviews with <u>successful users of direct response advertising, leading experts and entrepreneurs in direct marketing, and famous business authors and speakers</u>. Use them to turn commuting hours into **"POWER Thinking" Hours.**

★ **The New Member No B.S. Income Explosion Guide & CD** (Value = $29.97)

  This resource is <u>especially designed for NEW MEMBERS</u> to show them HOW they can join the thousands of Established Members **creating exciting sales and PROFIT growth** in their Business, Practices, or Sales Careers & Greater SUCCESS in their Business lives.

★ **Income Explosion FAST START Tele-Seminar with Dan Kennedy, Bill Glazer, and Lee Milteer** (Value = $97.00)

  Attend from the privacy and comfort of your home or office…hear a DYNAMIC discussion <u>of Key Advertising, Marketing, Promotion, Entrepreneurial & Phenomenon strategies</u>, PLUS answers to the most Frequently Asked Questions about these Strategies

★ **You'll also get these Exclusive "Members Only" Perks:**
  - **Special FREE Gold Member CALL-IN TIMES.**
  - **Gold Member RESTRICTED ACCESS WEBSITE.**
  - **Continually Updated MILLION DOLLAR RESOURCE DIRECTORY**

*There is a one-time charge of $19.95 in North America or $39.95 International to cover postage for 2 Issues of the FREE Gold Membership. After your 2-Month FREE test-drive, you will automatically continue at the <u>lowest</u> Gold Member price of $49.97 per month ($59.97 outside North America). Should you decide to cancel your membership, you can do so at any time by calling Glazer-Kennedy Insider's Circle™ at 410-825-8600 or faxing a cancellation note to 410-825-3301 (Monday through Friday 9am – 5pm). Remember, your credit card will NOT be charged the low monthly membership fee until the beginning of the 3rd month, which means you will receive 2 full issues to read, test, and **profit from all of the powerful techniques and strategies you get from being an Insider's Circle Gold Member.** And of course, it's impossible for you to lose, because if you don't absolutely LOVE everything you get, you can simply cancel your membership after the second free issue and never get billed a single penny for membership.

What is the Phenomenon™?

And How You Can Use It to Achieve More in Your Next 12 Months

Dan Kennedy
The Millionaire Maker
Creator of
The Phenomenon™

You're about to read about achieving more in the next 12 months than in the past 12 years. In case you're not familiar with me, my name is Dan Kennedy. My friends refer to me as "The Millionaire Maker." My track record spans 30 years including my own serial entrepreneur endeavors plus hands-on work in nearly 200 different types of businesses, including personal associations with hundreds of self-made, first-generation, from-scratch millionaire and multi-millionaire and 7-figure income entrepreneurs. Every year I influence more than 1 million entrepreneurs. People following my strategies frequently, even routinely, accomplish more in just 12 months than in the previous 12 years. In fact, this year not 1, but 2 of the companies on the prestigious Inc. Magazine list of the 500 fastest growing companies are owned by people who followed my lead and have experienced The Phenomenon™. To consult with me one-on-one is extremely expensive, yet 85% of all my private clients repeat.

You will notice the picture of the big sign that states, "But my business is different!" It is there as a reminder that thinking that your business

is different is a huge temptation, but it is also a huge roadblock to any progress. If you insist on paying attention only to ideas and information from your specific business you are guaranteed status quo, continuing to get the same results you get now. Most business owners and entrepreneurs are tempted to think this way. They only read their industry trade journals, only look at the other ads in their section of The Yellow Pages, only look at what their competitors are doing.

In the next 12 months big breakthroughs in sales, income, and growth are only possible for the business owner and entrepreneur who eagerly look at every effective idea to find something he can translate and transfer. Big breakthroughs occur when you look outside your specific business industry.

A Phenomenon™ is a thing that happens, and so when I was in my teens I first heard a success educator by the name of Earl Nightingale. If you don't know Earl I would recommend that you find some Earl Nightingale stuff and take a listen. I heard Earl on record, and he said 2 things, only 1 of which I'm going to talk about now, that had enormous impact. Earl said "There's a time in just about every entrepreneur's lifetime when the sun and the moon and the planets seem to align, and you're in the zone, in the groove and everything. When you attract more opportunity, more contacts, more cooperation, more resources, you make more money, you stack up more wealth, and you accomplish more of your goals in 12 months than you did in the previous 12 years." He didn't say it exactly this way, but I got the point. I stopped the record when I heard it and wrote it down because it was extremely encouraging at that particular moment in time to hear it.

What he didn't say – and I pretty much listened to every thing he ever recorded – what how to trigger it. It was encouraging to hear – to know that it happens, but it was not particularly useful because it happens, but now what? What do you do? Wait for it? Actually that's what most people do because it happens for most entrepreneurs organically, meaning that over a period of time they gradually get this piece put in place, this piece put in place, this piece put in place. Certain market conditions occur, and a whole bunch of factors converge and they have that experience. In many cases they have it, it occurred organically, they don't know why it happened, and they can't replicate it again on demand any more than they could make it happen on demand the 1st time. Knowing that it happens is encouraging but it's far more useful, of course, if there's a way to trigger it, to make it happen, and I didn't hear that.

Now over time here's what I've discovered. I've discovered that it happens. What he said was true. If you study, let alone going beyond the study, you'll find this moment in time, so the minute I heard it I was fascinated by it. I became more and more fascinated as time went on, and if you stop to think about it here's what's true of all of us: We are fascinated by speed, and we're frustrated by slow. America's the land of the microwave where we are exceedingly unhappy if it takes longer than 4 minutes to cook dinner. When I was a kid my parents had a TV which made you wait for it to warm up. We wait for nothing now. Speed happens all around us, but a lot of people haven't translated it into business and into making money. We're fascinated by speed. We're frustrated by slow.

Every one of you has this experience, as do I from time to time, our best intentions, our best ideas, they get all bollixed up in day-to-day routine, and what I view as the world's conspiracy against me. You have a world conspiracy against you, too, if you're an entrepreneur trying to get anything done. You get out of bed in the morning, and you race downstairs. You race to your place of business with your best of intentions, and then everybody tries to slow you down and that's what they do all day. There's this dichotomy in our lives between us trying to sort-of force speed to happen and everybody else sort-of being on slow. We know instinctively, if not experientially, that slow really doesn't work.

We have big plans for our business. You go home from a seminar with big plans for your business. If you try and implement them slowly what will happen to them? Think about what has happened to seminars you've been at before and gone home with great ideas, and tried to implement them slowly. If you have staff what does the staff try and encourage you to do when you come home with a lot of big ideas you want to act on? Move slowly; "We've got a lot of other things to do here." We know slow doesn't work. Slow is our enemy.

Yeah, we've been brainwashed that quick doesn't work. 'Get rich quick', for example, is a phrase that carries with it great negative stigma. I saw a consumer advocate on TV yesterday who was cheerfully telling everybody, "If it looks too good to be true it isn't, and if they're talking to you about getting rich quick run the other way." Here's what's important about that. All the training everybody gets comes from people who aren't rich and move slow. I always tell people, "Look, your brother-in-law may be a phenomenal person to get advice from about parenting. If he's got 5 kids all different ages, and they're all very well-behaved, and none of them are on drugs, and none of them are setting fire to the neighbor's cat, and he's just doing a great job as a parent by all means get parenting advice from your brother-in-law." That does not, however, mean that you should also get financial and business advice from your brother-in-law if he's got a $28,600.00 a year job, and he's had the same job for 22 years and it doesn't seem to be moving in any good direction, and he always needs to borrow money from you. See, he doesn't have it. He knows slow; and he knows 'get rich so slow it's never."

All the conditioning we've got about slow; all the speed limits have been set up by people who only know slow, but it doesn't work in business. It doesn't really work for the entrepreneur, and so a different approach is necessary. Here's what I know about The Phenomenon™, and I want to make the point that this is not just research or a book report. My life – I've been very fortunate in that a large part of my life, over 30 years, has been elbow-deep, intensely up close, personally involved with hundreds of 1st-generation, from scratch multi-millionaire and 7-figure income earning entrepreneurs. By 1st-generation I mean they are not members of the lucky sperm club. They started literally from scratch. In many cases their families maybe had small business but mostly were working-class people. So 1st-generation, from-scratch entrepreneurs started some kind of business, and turned it into something. Most of them are in the multi-millionaire and up category.

My personal work with them has yielded 2 things. The first is that The Phenomenon™ is real. What I heard about it originally is absolutely accurate. If you follow almost any entrepreneur over a 10, 20, 30, 40-year span of time in their entrepreneurial life they will have this 'in 12 months' experience where suddenly in 12 months they make more money, they create more wealth than in the previous 12 years. Even people who are already significantly successful have this occurrence. One of the people we've seen it happen to very, very visibly in recent years is Donald Trump. In the last handful of years Trump has had an experience far more broad and successful and wealth-producing and income-producing than probably in the previous 15 or 20. He has capitalized on it very, very well, so the 1st thing I can tell you is that it's real.

If you hang around long enough and you stick at it as an entrepreneur you're going to have one of these 'in 12 months' experiences that will occur for you organically. The 2nd thing I can tell you, which is much more useful, is that there actually are known strategies, known principles, known triggers that you can use to make The Phenomenon™ happen at will rather than waiting for it to occur organically and that you can use to extend it, so rather than it occurring for a very short period of time it occurs for an extended period of time. Perhaps most useful you can make it happen again and again and again because you will know why it has happened in the first place. Everybody's going to have the experience once if all they do is hang around and be an entrepreneur, but they're going to have the experience perhaps many times and when they want it if they closely examine the reasons why it occurs. In short, there are causes. It is an effect. You can let the causes occur organically or you can figure out what the causes are, and you can stitch them together yourself and you can manufacture The Phenomenon™.

The kind of people who have these experiences are the kind of people I work with. Let me just talk to you about some examples. These are all real people. In fact, I'll tell you in a minute how you can meet them. In this book you will meet somebody who went from actually living under a bridge – no exaggeration – to owning properties all throughout the city in which he lives. I have a personal client who I call 'The Disgusted Real Estate Agent' who dared to stop doing everything he hated about the real estate business (open houses, having the cell phone on, taking people around and showing them houses, doing listing presentations.) He stopped doing all of that and went from struggling to earning a million dollars a year.

I have a client who came from a really 'mean streets' kind of environment, started a small business slowly, and then went from 1 business to 5 businesses and over a million dollars worth of income in a 12-month period of time. I've got a guy 26 years old. He does something really interesting. He wakes up in the middle of the night with an idea; everybody does that. He wakes up in the middle of the night with an idea and does something about it, creates a business out of it, and in just 12 months he's got $300,000 from his business and goes on to develop a multi-million dollar business. Literally, not figuratively, from the steps of bankruptcy court in 12 months this guy launches a company and winds up having over 100,000 people literally standing in line getting financial advice from this former bankrupt. Another, after 8 years of plodding along earning a good living in a business, in one 12-month period he takes the business from local to national and 8 times his incomes.

Now these are representative, these are frankly typical, of the kind of people that I work with who all have Phenomenon™ experiences, manufactured Phenomenon™ experiences, not accidentally-occurring Phenomenon™ experiences. In the following pages, you hear these practitioners describe the triggers. Different people use different triggers to make The Phenomenon™ happen, so these are the people you meet. They are only representative of the hundreds and hundreds with whom I work on a regular basis, each of whom have been able to have a Phenomenon™ experience; in some cases more than one. In some cases sequential, serial Phenomenon™ experiences because they've learned how to trigger them.

Let me tell you what The Phenomenon™ is not. The Phenomenon™ is not theory, and it's not theory from theorists. This is not something somebody sat around and thought up in order to get a book out of it or get a speech out of it. This is something that really does occur in entrepreneurial life, but mostly occurs organically by accident but can be made to happen. It's not mysticism, and it's not a happy fuzzy fairy tale where somebody tells you what you want to hear. This is as practical as hammer and nails on a construction site. This book is about what you can do to make this happen.

Of late, as I'm writing this book, there's been a lot of talk about the law of attraction, and that's not what this is about either. I would say as an aside the law of attraction is not a law at all. Here's a law: gravity. Gravity is a law. You don't need to have an opinion about it. You don't have to think about it positively or negatively. As a matter of fact it even works on inanimate objects who have no thought process at all. If I drop the clock right now gravity will exert its law on the clock. The clock need not have a thought. The clock probably can't have a thought. Attraction is not that. Attraction is something that is made to happen. Attraction is a product of strategies, of thoughts, of actions, of behaviors, and it is part of The Phenomenon™ but not The Phenomenon™ in and of itself.

The secret is not in how you think. Thinking about it does not make it so, and so these are what I call lies of omission. They're true, but then they're not true because of what's omitted. One of the things I heard Earl Nightingale say that is not true because of omission is that we become what we think about most. Somebody said, "If that's true in about 10 minutes I'm going to be a girl." Well, funny, but obviously there's part of that that's not quite true, right? Napoleon Hill said, "Thoughts are things." I had somebody say to me about that, "Well, then where's my ham sandwich?" Arby's runs a commercial about this. Right now their advertising campaign is, "I'm thinking Arby's." Well, that thought is not a thing. Somebody still has to get in their car and drive over to an Arby's and get it, so it's true as far as it goes – thoughts can become things, but the error is in the omission.

The omission is what's really important to make The Phenomenon™ happen, so thinking does not make it so, certainly not what other people think. We know enough to ignore what other people think, and examples are historical and contemporary. I have a favorite example. Everybody told Walt Disney, "You can't have an amusement park with 1 entrance and 1 exit. It'll be a disaster." But Walt believed the key to the money being made was the 1 entrance, 1 exit so we can control the choreography of what you pass on your way in and on your way out.

I used to say when Sam Walton was alive if we bring Sam Walton up on stage, Donald Trump up on stage, and interview them both the list of differences is great: philosophical difference, personal appearance difference. Sam Walton was still driving around in his old pickup truck. Trump's got his name in 400-foot type on every vehicle, building, airline, person standing next to him, big ego; Walton, small ego, on and on. The differences are enormous. The only useful thing to find is the 3 or 4 commonalities, the 3 or 4 things or ways they think alike, and even more important, the 3 or 4 things they do alike. For example, they're both macro and micro, not one or the other so they're both concerned with little things in their business and big things in their business. There is congruent behavior, so we can figure out what the 3 or 4 or 5 or 7 or 12 things are that everybody who has a Phenomenon experience does leading up to it, and then we can make our behavior congruent with those X number of things. We will automatically create The Phenomenon™. There's resourceful behavior.

I was speaking many, many years ago on church marketing when a pastor of a mega church—you know, one of those churches with 4,000 or 5,000 people at a service. He said, "You know, if I mention a book then everybody wants to go to our bookstore and get that book. Then we have a real problem. 5,000 people, they go to a line up and buy these books. We only have so much square footage, and we only have so many people, and we only have so many cash registers. Then if people have to wait very long they get discouraged. They want to go do something else. They say to themselves 'I'll get that later' but they won't. Do you have any ideas for me?"

We were sitting at lunch, and I said, "Well, you know what comes to mind is the old drive-ins where they wore roller skates, and they had the little change belt. Hertz does it now. If you check in a Hertz car somebody comes out to the Hertz car, and they got the little thing on their belt. They process your check-in of the car right there. You don't have to go to the counter, so I said, "You know, maybe you could get a bunch of people and put them on roller skates with little credit card machines, and have them go up and down the lines and just run people's card and then send them to a pick-up window." Now, I was being funny. I thought I was entertaining myself putting on the Pastor.

Several months later I get the note and the picture of the people on the roller skates going up and down the lines taking the money. Reinvent the business for speed, right? It's a practical thing that you have to do, so whatever business you're in you've got to start to think about, "How can we get people to it faster? How can we get them through the sales process faster? How can we develop them as customers faster? How can we reinvent the business?" Radically change the way you work and are paid; that's part of embracing speed. Somehow you have to break free of dollars for hours. Somehow you have to break free of doing low-dollar value work in order to do more high-dollar value work, and give yourself permission to succeed fast. Now that's an emotional issue, so I have a quick story to tell you.

You have to able to give yourself permission for speed. Doing what would take 12 years in 12 months requires a mindset change for yourself and some immunity to the viewpoints of others. Another foundation for triggering The Phenomenon™ is modeling. If you know a lot of people who defy normal speed limits, and you're part of a group, and you're in an environment where you see it happening around you those models are very useful. If you have no models it doesn't mean you can't make this happen, but it's much more useful to have models. Linked to that is a support system, so it's very useful to have association of people who believe it is possible, understand it is possible, understand some of the principles and have had the experience themselves. That's why I encourage everybody to participate in coaching programs. That's why I encourage everybody to participate in mastermind groups. It's why I encourage people to find environments that they can put themselves in where people have had this experience, have this experience, know how to have that experience, and reinforce for them that they can have the experience.

Association is almost everything. It's very hard for us to immunize ourselves against slow if we are surrounded by slow. It's very hard for us not to get fast if we are surrounded by fast, so one of the great triggers for The Phenomenon™ is association.

Fast is better than slow, and so what you want to start thinking about is if you knew that you could make it happen in just 12 months what would you set out to do? What would you put on your list? What would you want to have happen in your business? That list would be dramatically different than the list you have now with the idea that it's going to be slow and arduous and painful to do certain things. What would your list look like if you knew it could happen for you in just 12 months? With The Phenomenon™ it can happen for you in just 12 months, just about anything you put on the list.

This book is your passport to a whole new and different world that will amaze, astound, intrigue, motivate, and benefit you as well as your business and your family. If you are ready to radically change the speed of your achievements then not only will you be thrilled about this adventure when you experience the first reading, but I know that you will want to read it several times to take notes and choose the strategies to act on personally, maybe even people to contact or opportunities to pursue. You'll be eager to share it with family members, friends, or business associates.

One little word of warning: This book will shake you up! It will cause you to question much of what you've believed to be facts about money and wealth and how it is actually attracted, about businesses and what really makes them successful, about accomplishing and achieving goals. This will rob you of a good night's sleep after reading it. It is frankly not for the faint of heart or anyone who actually prefers good excuses to achievement or security to liberty. If you are quite comfortable with your present pace this is not for you.

So, what goals would you set? What accomplishment would you seek? What income and status would you want? If you knew it could be yours in just 12 months. You undoubtedly have ideas, ambitions, goals, business, or life changes you'd really like to make but have felt beyond your reach, have suppressed, or back burnered feel slipping away from you. Surely if you knew there were strategies that could bring these things to life, to fruition, with speed you'd get them out of their hiding places and recommit to them, wouldn't you? This one of a kind book reveals little-known, boldly different speed strategies that may change everything for you just as they have for the people you meet in the book.

Don't let your true goals gather dust or be endlessly delayed and compromised. Get your next 12 months started now!

A few instructions before you begin the book...

There are entrepreneurs who've populated my audiences for two decades, subscribed to my "No B.S. Marketing Letter," and used my systems to transform ordinary businesses into extraordinary money machines that far, far out-perform their industry norms, peers, competitors, and their own wildest imaginations. How do they do it? The big switch is a simple one to state (more complex to do): they switch from traditional advertising to direct-response advertising. They stop emulating ordinary and traditional marketing and instead emulate direct marketing.

Entrepreneurial success, like most things in life, is mostly a matter of decision. A partnership, friendship, intimate relationship, or marriage that succeeds or fails, a book that gets written or remains a jumble of notes in a drawer, the garage that gets cleaned out Saturday or put off until next week – these are all the result of decision and determination to make the decision right. Making the right decisions is often a lot less important than determining to make your decisions right. Only by making a decision and acting on it can you get into action and move forward. By waiting to make only the perfect decisions, you remain inert and cannot move forward at all. To quote my friend, legendary ad man Gary Halbert: "Motion beats meditation."

Marketing "X"

From now on, every ad you run, every flyer you distribute, every postcard or letter you mail, every website you put up, every/anything you do MUST adhere to the following rules. To be fair, they are simplistic and dogmatic, and there are reasons to violate them in certain situations. But for now, sticking to them as a rigid diet will work. You can experiment later, after you've first cleansed your business of toxins

Rule #1: There will always be an offer or offer(s). My old speaking colleague Zig Ziglar always described salespeople who wimped out at the close as "professional visitors," not professional salespeople. From now on, you will be doing selling in print, selling with media, and you rarely want to be just a professional visitor – and in those rare times, by very deliberate intent, not accident. So, your task is to make a direct response offer. Which, fortunately, is simple. An offer is something like "buy this, get a 2nd one free" or "call for your free catalog and DVD". The more interesting and appealing the offer, the better, but the most important basic point is: never end a conversation in any media without making a direct offer.

Rule #2: There will be reason to respond tight now. My friend, top direct-response copywriter John Carlton, always advises imagining your prospective customer or client as a gigantic somnambulant sloth, spread out on the couch, loathe to move his sleeping bulk, phone just out of reach. Your offer must force and compel him to move now. Your goal is immediate response. A plain vanilla, dull, mundane offer won't do it.

Rule #3: Clear instructions. Two sub-rules: one, confused consumers do nothing. Two, most people do a pretty good job of following directions. Most marketers' failures and disappointments result from giving confusing directions or no directions at all. When you put together any marketing tool; ad, flyer, sales letter, website, phone script, etc., it should be a single focused path with high sidewalls to prevent the prospect from wandering off, that leads to a point of decision and action. At that point, you must tell the prospect exactly what you want him to do next, how and when, and what will happen as soon as he does. Stop sending out anything absent such clear instructions.

Rule #4: There will be tracking and measurement. You need real, hard facts and data to make good, intelligent marketing decisions. Making such decisions based on what you or your employees think is happening, feel, guess, have a sense of, etc. is stupid, and you don't want to be stupid, do you? Tracking means accurately collecting all the information you need to determine what advertising is working and what isn't, which offer is pulling and which isn't, what marketing has traction and what doesn't. Tracking leads to knowing what your return on investment is, for each dollar.

Rule #5: Branding as by-product. Traditional brand-building is fine for giant companies with huge budgets, vying for store shelf space and consumers' recognition. If you are the CEO of Heinz or Budweiser or some company like that, playing with other peoples' marbles, by all means, buy brand identity. Have fun. But if you are an entrepreneur investing your own marbles, then forget all about it. Focus on response and sales. If you develop brand recognition accidentally along the way, great. But do not spend even a dime solely and exclusively on creating it. Do not let trying to get it interfere with response.

Rule #6: There will be follow-up. I hate waste. People read your ad, call your place of business, ask a question, the receptionist answers it, and that's it – no capture of the caller's name, address, e-mail, etc., no offer to immediately send a free report, gift, coupons. That is criminal waste. It cost money to get that call. Doing nothing with it is exactly the same as flushing money down the toilet. Please go and do so, right now, so you internalize the feeling. Take the largest bill you have in your wallet, a $10, a $20, preferably a $100, go to your toilet, tear it in hunks, let them flutter into the toilet and flush. You probably won't like it. Good. Remember how much you don't like it every time you fail to follow-up (a lot) on a lead or customer.

Rule #7: There will be strong copy. Sales and subtlety rarely go hand in hand. There is enormous, overwhelming competition for attention, and clutter you must cut through. You can't send a shy, timid Casper Milk-toast guy out into the street to knock on a door of a home or walk into a business and beg in nearly a whisper for a few minutes of the prospect's time. So you can't do that with ad, flyer, letter, or postcard either. Send Arnold Schwarzenegger instead. He'll walk through the door. Be a commanding presence. He shows up, guy drops what he's doing and pays attention. Lots of the examples in this book and in the free gifts offered in this book show off very strong sales copy. Pay attention! Emulate examples like these. And I urge reading my book, *The Ultimate Sales Letter.*

Rule #8: In general, it will look like mail-order advertising. One of the most famous ad men in the world, who built one of the giant Madison Avenue agencies, David Ogilvy admitted that only us direct-response guys really know what we are doing; his guys were guessing. Who should you copy? Any and all ads for any business should mimic mail-order ads. I want you to get your hands on everything you can written and published by the following short list of people and study it as if your life depended on it:

- E. Joseph Cossman
- Gerardo Joffee
- Robert Collier
- Joe Sugarman

Also, Bill Glazer. He is a master at using mail-order style advertising. Any of the people I just listed would applaud bricks 'n mortar businesses. Accumulate a file of full-page newspaper and magazine ads that are mail-order ads, that ask you to buy or at least request free information, have a coupon or a toll-free number. Whenever you prepare or approve your ads, flyers, sales letters, websites, get out this file and compare. Yours better look like the ones in the file.

Rule #9: Results rule. Period. A lot of what you see in the remainder of this book will look or feel wrong to you. Too bold, too aggressive, too hype-y, too unprofessional, too whatever. Of course, that's the old you reacting to it, before you became a direct marketing pro. But, regardless of your experience in your business or even your expertise as a direct marketer, your opinions and feelings about your marketing don't count. You get no vote, because you don't put money into your cash register. Your spouse, momma, neighbor, golfing buddy, competitor or employee, don't get to vote either. For the same reason. Plus, the fact that they quite probably know zip about direct marketing. The only votes that get counted are the customers' or clients', and the only bona fide ballots are their checks or credit cards. Everything else is hot air. From now on, you will be the most results oriented businessperson on the planet. Immune to opinion, criticism or guesswork. If it sells, it's good. If it doesn't, it isn't.

Rule #10: You will be a tough-minded disciplinarian and keep your business on a strict direct marketing diet for at least six months. If you personally go on a diet, there are some things you need to do. First, purge your refrigerator and cupboards of fattening foods, junk foods. And keep them free of them. Celery sticks, not cookies. Second, decide on an eating plan and stick to it patiently and persistently. Third, get some tools, like a scale. Fourth, count something – calories, fat grams, carbs, Weight Watchers points, something, so you can subtract by the numbers, manage with numbers. Fourth, step up your exercise.

I sometimes get questions (complaints/excuses) – how can I use your kind of marketing when I don't have any money? The answer, incidentally, is manual labor – but as delivery mechanism, as in this example. Second, because we all hear liberals continually whining about the poor staying poor for lack of opportunity. There are lots of legitimate reasons to be poor. Virtually none to stay poor.

Keep these marketing principles in mind. Now let's hear from our Phenomenon™ practitioner so you can create your own Phenomenon™. Let's get started!

Best Opportunities Today for Chiropractors to Quickly and Easily Make More While Working Less Than Ever Before

Ben Altadonna

Phenomenon™ Experiences: The Phenomenon™ has enabled me to work from home, cabin, or coffee shop without a cell phone! Recently, I was invited to a small private dinner with Richard Branson and other entrepreneurs and ran a marketing meeting at the home of Ed McMahon. I am able to take my family and vacation among celebrities on secluded vacation properties and donate thousands of dollars to animal shelters, wildlife museum and refugees.

Phenomenon™ STATISTICS

1995: Dead broke, $60,000 in debt, living in my struggling chiropractic office, barely making enough for rent, food, and gas.

1996: Started implementing Phenomenon™ principles and within four months tripled my practice and started collecting $40,000 a month.

1997: My consulting and coaching career was born which boosted revenues exceeding twenty million dollars.

Opportunities for Success

I went from being a struggling chiropractor, living in my office, to owning a highly successful practice that attracted all the patients I could ever want. Over the last decade, I have built up quite a reputation in the chiropractic industry and am known as THE #1 NEW PATIENT ATTRACTION AUTHORITY, with close to 6,000 doctors worldwide as clients

I have many products including customizable marketing campaigns and newsletters to attract new patients and customers, as well as, direct response referral-generating products and strategies. I also do many seminars each year.

Getting Started

For the first time in years, more people are exiting the chiropractic field than entering it. College tuition costs are at an all time high. It is not unusual for students graduating with debt exceeding $100,000 - $150,000. Some graduates immediately fail at practicing, exit the profession, and default on their student loans.

As I share the principles of The Phenomenon™ with my clients, they first experience an immediate change in their attitude and awareness of what is possible; instantly recognizing the self imposed and industry imposed false beliefs. After that, within 30 to 120 days, they discover how to work more "on" their practice and less "in" their practice making more money, working less, and having a lot more leisure time for their family or hobbies. In just twelve months, I've witnessed many practices more than double in profit without necessarily having to double the volume of business or hours in the office. After experiencing The Phenomenon™, I've had several doctors from small and large cities do well over a million dollars in revenue a year.

Life and Business Today

Life is so much different now. I work at home when I want and can literally work where I want. I'm often seen at the coffee shop with my laptop. I'm now forty-six and can easily retire today without having to work another day of my life if I want, but this stuff is so much fun, I plan on working part-time for a long time; continuing teaching others about The Phenomenon™. For them and me, the money and fun is just too darn good.

Turning Points

The Phenomenon™ can change your life without changing who you are as a person. You can continue to live with ethics, integrity, and help others along the way without stepping on anyone while you rise to the top. Life and business are games but unlike most games, we really can change the rules anytime we want; if you practice the principles of The Phenomenon™, there are no boundaries only shortcuts to success and happiness.

Systems and Strategies

The biggest benefit of what I do is seeing my clients lives change practically overnight; the joy in their faces when they discover that they no longer need to worry about their futures. That they have control. They know how to reinvent themselves and their business and can activate these skills at will. They no longer view the passing of time as a factor in getting what they want.

Make More Money

Some of my doctors choose to work three days a week and make up to $25,000 a month or more, while others choose to make $50,000 to $200,000 a month. It is a choice, a decision. Once they make the decision to implement The Phenomenon™, they have a much greater chance of achieving levels of success that most people can't even comprehend.

Taking the First Step

First, I show doctors how to find and attract THEIR IDEAL PATIENT, and in essence, REPEL all the rest. That way, there is virtually NO wasted effort on prospective patients who are not ideal. I show doctors how to train their patients to pay, stay, and refer without the doctors feeling like a high-pressured used car salesmen. I teach my clients how to first decide exactly how much they want to make, how much they want to work, and how to come up with the simplest way to achieve their dream practice and how to make it happen in twelve months or less. My clients do not settle for anything less than exactly what they want. They know what to do and how to do it. It's that simple.

The Phenomenon™ Applied

The Phenomenon™ governs practically everything I do. It is congruent with everything good. It is a way of thinking. It is NOT religion. It IS about knowing what you want, and doing only things that get you closer to your goals. It is about building successful businesses FAST, managing time, managing expectations of others, and about personal responsibility.

The Next 12 Months

The Phenomenon™ is about establishing win-win situations. Give someone what he or she wants and you can have what you want. In the next twelve months, a person can go from subsistence to wealth, from depression to fulfillment. All you have to do is first know what you want; it doesn't matter if you know what you need to get there. For many, this is the hardest part, which is where The Phenomenon™ comes in.

You will learn how to get more out of each day. You will be more aware of time and opportunities. You will react differently to things that happen in your life and business, good and bad. You will say "no" to things you used to say "yes" to and "yes" to things you never thought you were worthy of.

The Phenomenon™ is a way of thinking so you can get more done in less time and effort. It will show you how to make yourself more valuable to others so that they will want what you have to offer and gladly pay top dollar for it. Take action! There is no such thing as failure or success; merely results.

10 Steps to Success

STEP 1: Have clearly defined, written goals with clearly defined action steps and deadlines to achieve each any and every one of them. Know and write down exactly what you want in business and in life.

STEP 2: Do what most people aren't willing to do. Most people aren't willing to get up one hour earlier and go to bed one hour later for those two extra, undisturbed hours each day. Do this and you will accomplish more in those two hours than you will the rest of the day.

STEP 3: Choose what you spend your time on. What you spend your time on is more important than how much work you actually do. Time is the most valuable commodity you have; yet, it takes little observation to see most people spend most of their time doing the most unproductive things – personally and professionally.

STEP 4: Don't confuse activity with achievement. Don't measure the value of what you do by how much time it took to do it. Spend the majority of your time doing the things that are going to yield the maximum results.

STEP 5: Delegate, delegate, delegate. Your job is to create work for others, not yourself. Leverage is how you build wealth. If you do anything that can be done for twenty dollars or less by someone else, then you will never get rich.

STEP 6: Don't complain. No whining. Nobody really cares and it creates more problems than it solves. People are attracted to winners. Winners don't complain. When things don't go your way, suck it up and immediately get into the "Here's what I'm going to do about it" mode. Don't let anyone see you sweat!

STEP 7: Surround yourself with successful people. Gladly pay for access. If there is someone you want to know; someone who knows something that is of value to you or someone you want to build a relationship with, pay for their time, buy them dinner, and don't ask for favors. Be humble but confident. Thank them for their time then follow up with letter and a gift.

STEP 8: Don't quit right at the goal line. Don't march eighty yards down the field and fumble at the moment of truth. Do the little extra it takes to get the touchdown and all the glory – that last and most important five percent.

STEP 9: Always be clear about why you do what you do: It's not a question of if things are going to get hard and ugly, it's a question of when. And when times get hard and ugly you need to have an awfully good reason to keep moving forward. Know why you do what you do.

STEP 10: Don't ignore your health. If you aren't disciplined to eat right and exercise seven days a week, then you might be rich someday but you won't be healthy and isn't that what it's all about?

* * *

Ben Altadonna is known for proving to doctors that practice-building is about identifying segments of the population who are already most likely to want care immediately, then attracting only these niche patients. Using his secrets, strategies, and support, Ben shows doctors that to work on their practice more than in their practice is the only way to get out of the "time for money" trap so they can do and earn more while working less. He is the man who has led thousands of doctors and business owners to achieve amazing marketing results with his "out of the box" approach and result-oriented coaching programs, Ben has experienced The Phenomenon™ several times throughout his career but never by accident. See just how he did it and what we can all learn from him and his amazing story.

Doctors Of Chiropractic!
Experience "The Phenomenon™" In Your
Practice And In Your Life RIGHT NOW...

For Doctors Who Enjoy Their Practice, Love Their Life, AND Would Be Tickled Pink Collecting $25,000 A Month Working 3 Days-A-Week... Without Any Val Pac, Newspaper, TV, or Radio Advertising Or Equipment Needed! None At All!

Simply Go To
BenAltadonna.com
And Discover For Yourself...

#1. The ability to make just a little more money ($5,000-$15,000 more a month) for savings and to enjoy life.

#2. To relax at night and on weekends without ever talking, thinking, promoting, or worrying about the practice.

#3. To buy a house or a little larger house and maybe a safer or bigger car for the family.

#4. To increase referrals without begging.

#5. More time to do meaningful things like at least one big vacation per year, free time to do the fun things life has to offer, and if possible, maybe even take every Friday off.

#6. Clear and uncomplicated "exit strategy"...so that some day the systematized and very profitable practice can be sold quickly and simply...for all cash.

#7. The #1 mistake your C.A. is making every day that is costing you 3-5 new patients and thousands of dollars in cash per month!

#8. What to give every new patient the moment they walk in your practice for the very first time.

#9. The "Ascension Model"...The importance of having the answer to the question, "What's next?" for every patient.

#10. What to do RIGHT NOW!...with all those old patient files!!!... that will create an immediate cash surge in just 14 days or less!

#11. What patients really want to hear from you…you'll be shocked how many expensive mistakes you are still making!… And how easy it is to correct it!

#12. NO MORE STRESS OR GUILT WHEN YOU AREN'T WORKING!

Discover for yourself why over 6,000 Doctors Worldwide Use Ben's Practice, Lifestyle, & Wealth Building Strategies!

Experience
"The Quantum Leap Alliance™"
Go To: www.BenAltadonna.com

Best Opportunities Today for Anyone, from Garbage Man to CPA, to Quickly and Easily Build a Highly Profitable College Planning Business

Ron Caruthers

Phenomenon™ Experiences: It's happened twice. First, when I took my college planning business and added additional services, like offering mortgages to my clients and other financial services like retirement and inheritance planning, and a service to help my clients buy houses for their student children. Then, it started happening again as I added coaching and information marketing to the mix.

Phenomenon™ STATISTICS

2004 – Doing well with a college planning business grossing $490,000.

2005 – Added the additional services, mortgage and a real estate division, and took it to a $2 million dollar business in only 7 Months! (Keep in mind this was ALL on the same number of existing clients.)

2006 – Added coaching, a now seven-figure business which will reach about 5 million in revenue next year.

2007 – Added a do-it-yourself college planning information business. The numbers aren't complete yet, but that will generate between 8 and 10 million a year. Shooting for 20 million by 2009.

Opportunities for Success

I provide a complete turnkey, paint by numbers system to help anyone that's willing to work and learn to build a college planning business from scratch that will allow them all the time off they could wish for, provide them with an income that puts them in the top 5% of society, gives them stability, and gets them a clientele that will be almost rabid in their loyalty and devotion.

In just 12 months, any diligent, hard-working student can set up a practice that will pay for all the toys they could ever desire, allow them all the free time they could possibly use, AND give them prestige and respect in the community like they've never experienced before. Oh yeah, and they should be making a six-figure net income that is as predictable and dependable as the sun rising each morning, and because people are always going to go to college no matter what the housing market, stock market, or interest rates are doing, this business will never experience the ups and downs that other businesses have.

Turning Points

- Finding out that the market will happily bear much higher prices than I had been charging.
- Finding the 'business hidden within the business.' In our case, it turned out to be the mortgage and real estate company that was buried inside our college planning business and realizing that we were sitting on an untapped gold mine. Now, we're working on a legacy planning company for the grandparents of our students.
- Speed wins. I've learned to not be afraid of making a huge mess and then cleaning it up later. Just like an airplane will never get off the ground until it hits rotation speed, I've spent many years driving up and down the runway, as it were, without ever going fast enough to actually get airborne.

Achieving Success

The BEST thing to have in business, besides a starving audience, is a proven system for attracting clients, a proven system for retaining clients – keeping them happy – and a proven system for getting them to refer ALL of their friends and family to you, which is exactly what I provide for my coaching clients. I've laid out every step for them based on my fourteen years of experience doing this business.

The Next Step

The easiest way to learn more about what I offer is to go to www.roncaruthers.com/Phenomenon™. In a nutshell, what I offer is a complete turnkey, paint by numbers system to help anyone build a college planning business from scratch that will allow them to leave the frustrations of a changing marketplace behind and start generating an income that puts them in the top 5% of society. How I do this is by offering them everything they could possibly need: marketing, support and a PROVEN system that is fail proof if carried out just as I show you.

The Phenomenon™ Applied

My take is that it is a process that all super-successful people go through at some point in their life that launches them from ordinary income to extraordinary amounts of wealth, and where opportunities begin to present themselves that just months earlier would have been unimaginable. For instance, I think of Donald Trump, who always had a measure of fame, after "The Apprentice" started airing, and all of the sudden, he has his name on clothing, water bottles, perfume, vodka (he doesn't even drink!) and anything else you can name or think of. It extends way beyond his previous real estate ventures.

The Next 12 Months

Completely reinvent yourself by getting a makeover on your lifestyle and income and allow yourself to live a life that you now probably only dream of. From paying off debts to putting money in the bank, to supporting family members that can't support themselves, to getting the car you've always wanted, to buying the dream house or the second house you've always wanted. PLUS, you get the added benefit of having a unique skill set that millions of people are looking for and will respect you for like they would a top heart surgeon. Success is not only possible, it is predictable and inevitable, if you're willing to follow the steps that I lay out and go to work.

My opportunity may or may not be right for everyone, although for the right person it will be like a dream come true. The principles behind The Phenomenon™ are timeless and will work for anyone, no matter what arena you choose to practice them in. So, my advice is to study the opportunities before you, pick one, and then put your head down and your butt up and get to work. Be a diligent, relentless student of what you choose to master and force it to happen in your own life.

10 STEPS TO SUCCESS

STEP 1: Intelligently pick your opportunities. There are only so many hours in the day, so start by making a list of everything that you hate, and make sure that what you choose to invest your time in allows you to avoid as many of those as possible.

STEP 2: What you say no to is even more important than what you say yes to. Again, you're better off selecting one or two opportunities and really digging in and getting good at them rather than trying to tackle everything at once.

STEP 3: Fish where the fish are. Make sure there is an audience for what you are doing *before* you invest time or money.

STEP 4: Fish where the fish are starving. Look for things where people are passionate and driven by their emotions of greed, pride, fear, guilt and love. Link your business to people's passions (in my case, their kids) and you'll have them lining up to get to you.

STEP 5: Do something to get new business every day. A good habit that I learned from Dan Kennedy is to do at least one thing every day to fill your pipeline of new business. There is a link between this behavior and experiencing The Phenomenon™

STEP 6: Be a true student of your business. Study everything you can get your hands on, both in terms of books, articles and other people that are successful in your field.

STEP 7: Study marketing. You must become a master student of marketing to be able to attract more clients than you could possibly work with. This allows you to command premium prices, have a halo effect around your business, and being able to personally pick and choose who you want to work with.

STEP 8: Set rules regarding access to you that both your staff and clients have to follow. Avoid the trap of being a slave to your e-mail and cell phone. Make yourself more valuable by being somewhat inaccessible. This will allow you time to plan and think.

STEP 9: Work really, really hard…especially in the beginning when you're getting started.

STEP 10: On the other hand, make sure that you build "down time" into your schedule. Be sure to build in time in your weekly schedule to exercise, goof off with your family, engage in a hobby or whatever else revitalizes and recharges you. Remember my rule: work until you're exhausted; then play until you're bored.

* * *

Ron Caruthers is a college planner, assisting families with every aspect of sending a child to college. He teaches at Palomar and Mira Costa Colleges on college planning and is the author of Help Your Kid Get Ready for College and How to Get Thousands of Dollars for Your Child's Education. A regular guest on KUSI TV news in San Diego, he has also been a guest on many radio stations throughout the country. He has helped over 1550 families send their kids to colleges that they never thought they could afford, and doing so in a way that leaves them in better financial shape then he found them. Ron has been married just shy of twenty years to Kathryn. They have three kids and reside in Carlsbad, California.

Are YOU Ready To Take CONTROL Of Your Business and Your Future...Have Clients Coming To You... CUT Your Work Time in HALF and Start Living The Lifestyle You Have Always Dreamed About

I know what your thinking...too good to be true right? Wrong! Let me prove it to you. I want to send you a GIANT **10 Pound Box of Goodies**. That's right. Over $494.00 worth of FREE stuff that will show you *exactly* what I offer... PLUS a peek at my own personal business plan.

So let me send you:

- **2 DVD**'s- one detailing the financial aid system and How my College Planning Client Attraction System' works...how the money is made and how we can attract more clients that you will know what to do with. (a $98.00 value)

- 2 CD's- #1 is Dan Kennedy and Bill Glazer interviewing me on Selling to the Affluent, and how we structure our pricing to maximize profits AND to attract a premium, high end clientele. (people paid $247.00 per seat to hear this...you can't find it anywhere else) #2 is a tele-conference I did on The Phenomenon™ Experience (we charged $99 for this call and you get it FREE!)

- 3 Books- No BS Wealth Attraction for Entrepreneurs from Dan Kennedy and two of my own: Help Your Kid Get Ready for College and How to Get Thousands of Dollars for Your Child's Education. (together worth over $50)

- Plus several articles and a peek at my business plan.

So are you ready to experience The Phenomenon™ for yourself?

Here are 3 easy ways to get started and get your BIG Box of FREE stuff worth over $494.00:

1. Call my office at 760-438-9095 and leave your name and mailing address and mention you heard about this in The Phenomenon™

2. Complete the form below and fax to 760-438-5232

3. Or simply visit www.roncaruthers.com/Phenomenon™

____YES Ron, I want to receive your FREE Big Box of Goodies that will show me exactly how I too can build a MILLION Dollar College Planning business, as well as tons of useful and use

Name_____

E-mail Address_____

Street Address_____

_____

City_____ **State**____ **Zip Code**_____

Work Phone_____

Fax Number_____

Your Company's Name_____

_____

Are you an Agent or Broker? Agent Broker?_____

What market do you operate in?_____

_____

How Anyone of Any Background, Any Education, Living Anywhere Can Quickly and Easily Create a Highly Successful Internet Business in 12 Months or Less

Derek Gehl

Phenomenon™ Experience: I have had two major Phenomenon™ turning points in my life. First, when I met Cory Rudl in 1998 and was introduced to the incredible world of opportunity in Internet marketing, and again in 2003 when I was introduced to the legendary Dan Kennedy and implemented his offline techniques into my online world. Results were truly amazing!

Phenomenon™ STATISTICS

1998 – With a $25 investment started Internet Marketing Center with Corey Rudl, sales at that time, less than $1,000,000.

2003 – Implemented Kennedy marketing techniques, sales jumped from $6.64 million to $11.39 million in just over 12 months.

2006 – My biggest year ever with $20,000,000 in 2006 alone. Sold over $70,000,000 on the Internet, have over 100,000 customers, 200,000 affiliates, and 800,000+ subscribers – and growing.

Future – $100,000,000 per year in the next 5 years.

Opportunities for Success

My firm currently provides the most comprehensive training system that takes complete beginners through the process of building a wildly successful business on the Internet. Many call it "The Insiders Secrets to Marketing Your Business on the Internet." We have been selling this system since 1997, which makes it the longest running and one of the best know systems online today. The beauty of the Internet is how easy it is to get started. For only a few hundred dollars, you can be up and running on the Internet with a fully functional web business making money.

Getting Started

When I finished high school, I looked around for the "next big thing" and at that time I found the Internet. Knowing very little about computers, I took a few courses and built a few websites and started to dabble. I saw that what people were doing was truly phenomenal! There were millionaires being created daily and I knew I wanted to be part of it.

Now, there are people in this world that believe in fate and there are people that believe you control your destiny. I am a believer in both. I think everyone will be presented with some great opportunities in life but it is up to you to take action and make something out of them. So, this is the fate part. In early 1998, by chance, I met a gentlemen by the name of Corey Rudl who at that time was five years my senior at the ripe old age of twenty-five. He had the same interest in the Internet and was a few steps ahead of me building his business online…he was already a millionaire! In fact, he was so success-ful that when I met him he had just developed his own Internet marketing course to teach other people how to build their businesses online.

To say the least, this was one of those opportunities I had in my life where I had a choice! I could continue doing what I was doing or I could learn from someone who had already seen the success I wanted to achieve. So, I did everything I could and convinced this Internet marketing genius to take me under his wing and mentor me. It is not something he had ever done, but I knew I wanted it. I was persistent, offered him enough value, and he agreed!

And the rest you could say is history! Well almost… From there, we built what is now The Internet Marketing Center from a two-man shop into a massive organization, with well over a hundred incredible employees, cus-tomers all over the world and a track record of helping more people create massive success on the Internet than any other company I know of.

Business Today

Unlike many entrepreneurs, I like to build businesses and I want to make it as big as possible. My goal is $100,000,000 per year in the next five years and we have the plan to do that. That said, many entrepreneurs like to keep their business small and create more of a lifestyle business, which we could have done but that is not my personality.

So business-wise my life is an adventure. One day, I will be writing a sales letter for our next big promotion or brainstorming with my development team to design a cutting edge marketing application, and the next day, I could be in Europe speaking to thousands of people about how to build a business online. An adventure, indeed!

The Next 12 Months

In the next twelve months people could increase their income by thousands of dollars every month. I have seen this accomplished time and time again. There is no one answer I can give because it depends on ones commitment to achieving their goals, but the most important thing I can say it that it does happen. The success stories are real folks just like you and if you plug into a proven system like mine you can have a success story of your own in a few short months.

Words of Wisdom

So if you ask me how was my Phenomenon™ possible? The answer is simple. I did three things:

1. When presented with an opportunity, I took action and NEVER took "no" for an answer.
2. Found incredible mentors and studied them intensely.
3. And never stopped learning.

These three qualities are what I believe sets phenomenal people apart from the rest of the world. Now, the choice is yours.

8 Steps to Grow a Hugely Profitable Internet Business... Without Breaking the Bank!

STEP 1: Find a hungry niche market - BEFORE you decide what to sell. The fact is: most people do NOT go online to buy. They go online looking for information or to solve a problem. What you need to do is find an untapped niche market; a group of people who are going online to solve a common problem, but are not having any luck finding a solution. Once you've found a hungry niche market and come up with a product that will satisfy their wants, it's time to write your sales copy...

STEP 2: Write compelling sales copy that draws in your visitors. Without a doubt, the most important part of your website is your sales copy. It's the only contact most of your visitors are going to have with your business — so you have to make sure it does the job of a top performing salesperson.

STEP 3: Design a winning site that converts visitors into buyers. The most important thing to remember when designing your sales website is KEEP IT SIMPLE! You only have ten seconds when someone arrives at your website to grab their attention -- otherwise, they're gone, never to be seen again.

STEP 4: Use the Net's top search engines to drive tons of targeted traffic to your site. There are two ways to use search engines to drive traffic to your site: Using pay-per-click (PPC) programs like Google AdWords and Yahoo Search Marketing, and getting ranked in the "organic" search engines.

STEP 5: Tap into secret sources of cheap (and even free!) traffic. As an online marketer, one of your most important assets is your reputation. People need to know who you are, and why they should trust you! So how do you "spread the good word" about you and your business to the far corners of the Web? Easy! You can give away free content by writing articles and submitting them to online article directories, issue press releases about your business and become an active expert in industry forums.

STEP 6: Use the power of e-mail marketing to keep in touch with your visitors – and turn them into buyers! It takes an average of four to seven contacts with someone before they will be comfortable enough to buy something from you, so you need to stay in touch with your visitors and build a relationship with them. E-mail marketing is the ideal way to do this.

STEP 7: Grow your business by selling new products to your existing customer base. It's a little-recognized fact that at least 36% of people who have purchased from you once will buy from you again IF you follow up with them. Stay in regular touch with your customers and let them know about new products you have available.

STEP 8: Harness the power of affiliate programs for hands-free traffic and sales! Once you have a profitable business on your hands, you should always be on the lookout for new ways to grow it. And one of the best ways to do that is to launch your own affiliate program. Affiliates are people who promote your products on their website for a cut of the selling price.

* * *

Derek Gehl is the 30-year-old internet marketing "over-achiever," who has led thousands to achieve mind-blowing results with his Internet marketing training systems and programs. He is the CEO of Internet Marketing Center, a company with over a hundred employees dedicated to helping individuals build massive success on the Internet. He has helped create more success stories on the Internet than any other company in the world..

Are You Ready To Learn The "Real" Internet Marketing Secrets That Will Have You Making More In The Next 12 Months Than You Have In The Last 12 Years?

For Just $2.95 You Too Can Discover the Step-By-Step System that Turned a $25 Investment on the Internet to $60 Million in Sales!

Don't miss out on the **PROVEN** system that has generated

HUGE profits on the Web for people just like YOU!

You must act quickly…**OFFER EXPIRES IN 30 Days!**

Get UNLIMITED access to my e-business success training system, the "Insider Secrets to Marketing Your Business on the Internet", for only $2.95 for the next 30 days.

EVERYONE -- Students, grandparents, nurses, carpenters, accountants, stay-at-home parents, stunt men, cattle farmer, alligator wranglers, firemen, sanitation engineers, doctors, musicians, landscaper, and the list could go on... can put this PROVEN success system to work!

I have helped countless people, from all walks of life, build successful, profitable business on the Internet... even complete internet beginners. There is only one thing they all had in common - **they took action!**

If you can spare $2.95, you can spend the next 30 days using my $60 Million advantage to learn how to start a wildly lucrative Internet business and make an EXTRA $7,500 to $12,750 every month, working as little as 30-60 minutes per day...

Take me up on this incredible offer (before I come to my senses) and get your very own copy of this #1-rated Internet wealth system... **ALL for just $2.95!**

Simply go to **www.marketingtips.com/tipsltrphen.html** and you can have access to this life changing information immediately! No risks...no funny stuff, just the info that will get you one step closer to achieving The Phenomenon™ in your life!

Learn the Secret to Building a WILDLY Successful Commercial Real Estate Business...More Money, Less Work in 12 Months or Less

Jim Gillespie

Phenomenon™ Experience: In 1994, I was a successful commercial real estate broker but was dealing with the worst real estate market since the Great Depression in Los Angeles. Times were difficult and then everything hit the fan and completely changed the way I looked at life and lived it. I could have let all of this completely suck me down the drain. Instead, I chose to reframe what all of it meant in a way that would empower me and my entire future.

Phenomenon™ STATISTICS

1979-1998 – Successful commercial real estate broker bringing in a solid, six-figure income.

1998 – Began coaching and training which doubled and then tripled his income.

Present – Currently getting paid $1,200 an hour for coaching and consulting with commercial real estate professionals.

Future – After implementing his new coaching and training programs within the next several months he expects income to grow by at least 40%.

Getting Started

I tell commercial real estate agents: "The all-important underlying ingredient that you must bring to the table is your incredible passion and love for the commercial real estate brokerage business and your unyielding drive to be hugely successful at it. This is the engine that completely drives your success."

I find that the people who achieve huge success in any business are the ones who want it the most and are unwilling to let anything stand in the way of having it. Achieving great success in commercial real estate brokerage isn't easy. You have to have the right stomach for it and tremendous resiliency. And you have to be able to tolerate wide mood swings, as some days you'll feel on top of the world and on other days you'll feel like the world is on top of you. This is because the excitement of generating new transactions and the disappointment of having some transactions fall apart on you are all a normal part of your week-to-week business in commercial brokerage.

Business Today

I live about one hour inland from San Diego and about ninety minutes from Downtown Los Angeles. I had gotten to the point where I was tired of the commercial brokerage business and I wanted a change. So I reinvented myself and created a brand new career as a commercial real estate coach. No one in the industry had ever done commercial real estate coaching before; and I was the one who created it.

I work from home, I coach people on the phone, I do live telephone seminars, and coaching programs. I sell commercial real estate agent training products through my website, and I publish a free commercial real estate training E-newsletter that's read by more than 20,000 people. I enjoy my life much more now because I really love teaching people and helping them to be better at what they do, and make more money.

Turning Points

First of all, my parents were both wonderful, loving people, and very honest and ethical. They allowed me to develop into the person I wanted to become, and were very supportive in everything I did. This created an important foundation for me to move forward in my life from. In 1985 I attended my first ever personal development seminar and the instructor said to everyone, "The only difference between you and the person who has everything you want in your life, is they didn't buy the reasons you have for not having those things. You either have what you want in life or you have the reasons why you don't."

That quote just spun my head around and made me realize that having what I wanted was completely up to me; I choose what happens in my life.

So what happened in my life in 1994? My father died, I went through a divorce, began taking care of my mother whose Alzheimer's disease had progressed, and had to take care of my sister with schizophrenia. It was a major turning point as I decided I would use all the pain I was feeling to transform my life into the unimaginable – and not let all of this pain suck me down the drain.

Becoming a Master Practitioner and Trainer of NLP (Neurolinguistic Programming), Hypnotherapy, and Time Line Therapy made me realize how much I would love working with people to help them transform their lives, and it gave me some great tools to work with people, too.

Money Making Strategies

I normally work with people making anywhere between $100,000 a year up to about $2,500,000 a year. I have one particular client who was making $250,000 a year after fourteen years in commercial brokerage, and last year he made $1,500,000 after his eighth year of working with me.

Two of my clients working as a team made an additional $500,000 in eleven months just through sending out mailers to their clients and prospects under my supervision and direction. I coached them on exactly what to do when designing and sending these mailers out to their people. You can read more stories if you go to my website www.realestatesalescoach.com/testimonials.htm

The Phenomenon™ Applied

From my own experience, The Phenomenon™ is about staying focused on what you want to have in your life and never, ever letting anything stop you from having it. Obstacles will always come up, along with some very difficult experiences. But if you stay focused on what you want and stay determined to have it more than anything, you will have what you want in your life.

The Next 12 Months

When I'm speaking in front of commercial real estate audiences, sometimes I'll ask the following question: "If you prospected 10-12 hours every week over the next year in your business, how much of a difference would this make in your income?" And about 60% of the audience will usually raise their hand and tell me they think they would double their income by doing this, about 20% think they would triple their income, and overall about 90% think they would increase their income by at least 30% over the next year. Oftentimes increasing one's income substantially has nothing to do with learning new ideas you've never heard of before. It's got more to do with focusing on implementing ideas you've learned before. But sometimes making more money does involve learning new skills and ideas and implementing them into your business.

Words of Wisdom

If more than anything else in the world you want to take your commercial real estate brokerage business to an entirely new level, you can definitely make it happen. But if you've been trying to take your business to a new level on your own and you've been stagnating, you're not seeing what you're doing wrong that's causing the problem. Get with someone who has great insight to show you what you're doing wrong and get you on the path to producing outstanding results in your business right away.

10 Steps for Success in Commercial Real Estate Brokerage

STEP 1: Pick the best company. Work for the commercial real estate brokerage company that's best for you. Work for the company that provides you with the right tools and makes it easier to get business with the people and companies you want to work with.

STEP 2: Prospect 10-12 hours every week, and prospect only the people and companies whose next transaction will be in the size range you want to work on.

STEP 3: Mail to every client and prospect you want to do business with two or more times every month, providing them information they'll want to know about. This keeps them thinking of you as the one knowledgeable advisor they'll want to work with when it's time for their next transaction.

STEP 4: Build strong, quality relationships with the people and companies you want to be working with. Great relationships have people hire you again and again as their commercial real estate broker, moving you towards your goal of becoming their "broker for life."

STEP 5: Socialize with the people you want to do business with. People want to work with others they feel are their friends, and socializing makes you feel more like a friend to them. In addition, it's more difficult for people to quit doing business with their friends.

STEP 6: Continually work on improving your presentation skills. This enables you to close more business with the leads you're already generating. Videotape your presentation for an exclusive listing with someone else role-playing as the person you want to have sign the listing. Then watch the videotape and notice what you learn.

STEP 7: Buy gifts for your clients 2-4 times every year. This creates the feeling of having more of an ongoing relationship between transactions with them, and maximizes the probability they'll work with you again on their next transaction. Investing about $1,000 in gifts over a five-year period to ensure working on a transaction that will pay you $20,000 is a great investment.

STEP 8: Position yourself as the best agent in your territory. Create this image of you in your advertising, marketing, and through testimonials. Then people will naturally feel more compelled to work with you over your competitors.

STEP 9: Invest your own money into improving your real estate business. Many agents don't want to spend any of their own money on developing their real estate business, and this is a huge mistake. Invest in the tools, software, mailing, and marketing programs that will bring you more business, and spend money on gifts and on socializing with your clients even if your company won't pay for it.

STEP 10: Commit to your ongoing continuing education and training. Many agents don't believe in this and they just keep producing the same old results in their real estate businesses year after year. Invest in coaching to get you to implement great new changes and strategies into your real estate business.

* * *

Jim Gillespie is known as America's Premier Commercial Real Estate Coach℠. He's the founder of Advanced Commercial Real Estate Coaching, a company that trains, coaches, and speaks to commercial real estate brokers, their managers, and the principals of commercial real estate brokerage companies. Jim's personal interests include learning, reading, personal and spiritual development, meditation, and studying American History. He's constantly working to improve himself through attending seminars, watching DVDs, and listening to audio CDs about business and marketing.

Are You Ready To Learn The Secrets To Building a WILDLY Successful Commercial Real Estate Brokerage Business That Will Have You Making More In The Next 12 Months Than You Have In The Last 12 Years?

Get 2 Months of
My Million Dollar Commercial Real Estate Agent
Inner Circle Program
(a $594.00 value)
FOR FREE!

Here's What You Can Expect:

- **Two months of direct access to my monthly telecoaching training sessions**, "The Gillespie Method: The 12 Power Steps to Explode Your Commercial Real Estate Commissions", specifically for commercial real estate agents.
- Two months of **direct access to ask me any question you want** to on how to successfully take your commercial real estate brokerage business to the next level. This question and answer session will take place at the end of each month's teleconference.
- An **audio CD** recording of each month's teleconference sent to you in the mail.

- A **written transcription** of each month's teleconference sent to you in the mail.

- A one-page highlight sheet of each month's teleconference sent to you in the mail.

- **Direct access to call me during my special monthly call-in times.** I set aside two hours every month for my Inner Circle members to reserve one-on-one telephone coaching appointments with me. And if you reserve an appointment I'll work with you on your real estate business for 10 minutes. This is on a first-come first-served basis for Inner Circle members who take action every month and reserve appointments with me immediately when I make them available.

All of this together represents a normal value of $594, but through this Special Offer you'll receive all of these benefits for two months for FREE! You just cover the shipping and handling of $19.95 US/Canada ($29.95 for all other countries) ...that's right $594.00 worth of guaranteed business building info for only $19.95 shipping and handling! No other costs... no other fees.

But Here's The One Catch...

This offer is ONLY for those people currently working full-time in commercial real estate brokerage. This program is not for the beginner, but instead is completely focused on teaching intermediate and advanced level commercial agents how to skyrocket their income and achieve The Phenomenon™ in both their own life and business.

To sign up for this two-month free trial offer go to www.realeastatesalescoach.com/innercircle.htm

How Any Independent Retailer Can Discover the Hidden Wealth in Their Retail Business and See Increased Sales of 20, 50%, Even 100% within 12 Months or Less

Bill Glazer

Phenomenon™ Experiences: In 1995, I traveled from Baltimore to Philadelphia to attend an all day seminar featuring top speakers such as Zig Ziglar, Tom Hopkins, Former U.S. President Ronald Reagan, Jim McCann, and legendary marketing guru, Dan Kennedy. When I heard Dan speak about ways to cut all of the fat and waste in marketing dollars and apply measurable direct response techniques, I immediately applied it to my already successful retail stores with outstanding success. Then in 1997, I had a very fortuitous lunch with Dan that launched me into a second career as an advisor, consultant, and coach to the retail industry. In 2004, Dan asked me to join forces with him to create Glazer-Kennedy Insider's Circle™ which now provides marketing and money-making advice and tools to well over 100,000 entrepreneurs in every category of business throughout the globe.

Phenomenon™ STATISTICS

1995 – Operated two menswear stores in Baltimore, heard Dan Kennedy speak, applied his direct response strategies and achieved a 31% increase in business within the next 12-months.

1998 – Launched BGS Marketing to provide marketing systems to retail businesses. Over 500 retailers invested within the first year, generating over a million dollars in sales.

2004 – Joined forces with Dan Kennedy to create Glazer-Kennedy Insider's Circle. Experienced over a 500% increase in membership and sales within the first 12-months.

2007 – Provides marketing advice to 3,700 retailers and over 100,000 entrepreneurs. Publishes four monthly newsletters, speaks an average of 18-times a year, conducts four sold out events, facilitates different levels of coaching groups, and consults with a handful of elite private clients.

Opportunities for Success

I provide information to entrepreneurs, especially independent retail store owners, helping them make the mental shift from being the operators of their businesses to becoming marketers of their businesses. Most independent retail storeowners market by copying the marketing and advertising techniques of other retailers that are within their same category of business. This is what Dan Kennedy has termed "Marketing Incest." Businesspeople copy one another, rather than distinguishing themselves and their business.

What I teach people to do is what I call "S & D" marketing. This is what gave my own retail businesses a big leap in results. S & D stands for "steal and distribute," which is ethical theft that is taking from outside of your industry what's working and applying it to your own trade. For example, in 1999, I observed that within the mortgage industry they were using a technology called voice broadcasting. This is when you automatically leave messages on home answering machines about special opportunities. Although the rules have changed as to how you can legally use this technology today, back when I applied it to my retail business, I achieved a whopping ninety-two percent increase in sales during the same period the prior year.

Today, I offer my new and updated BGS Marketing System to retailers who are in search of the exact tools and strategies they can use for their businesses. Plus, in order to keep our members current, we also provide a monthly newsletter and CD interview series that exposes our members to the most up-to-date discoveries and reinforces important moneymaking principals. One of the shining jewels of our program is a state-of-the art loyalty program called Royalty Rewards that puts all of the strategies I teach on autopilot for our members. This program does all of the marketing from acquiring new customers, getting existing customers to return on average twice as often, and even getting what we call "lost customers" to return to the store. This program is so powerful that we provide retailers an unprecedented ninety-days to test-drive the entire program in order to begin experiencing The Phenomenon™ in their own business.

Getting Started

Opening a retail business is very labor and capital intensive. It demands a lot of time, energy, and resources. It's complicated – there's securing and building a location, purchasing inventory, hiring personnel, developing an accounting system, and getting your message out to the public.

The days of selling the best products and delivering an exceptional level of customer service and having the world beat a path to your door are over. You still have to do both of those things, but in the end, it's the best marketer who wins. Once people begin with my strategies, I've seen people experience double-digit increases in profits and sales within the first quarter of business. Best of all, with the correct system in place, within twelve months they can be working less, spending more time with their family, and taking vacations they haven't had in years.

The Early Years

I immediately joined the family business, which was a true family business. When I first began there were a total of nine employees consisting of my father, mother, two uncles, an aunt, three others, and myself. There were fourteen other menswear stores as well as four department stores in downtown Baltimore competing with us. Throughout the 70s and 80s I noticed that these stores were slowly closing up one at a time and I knew something was wrong. I began looking for answers within my industry and found out that menswear retailers were dropping like flies everywhere. The people who were conducting seminars at the industry trade shows were clueless and I later called these speakers who were presenting "pretend experts" because they taught principals that were in their dreams, but they never actually did any of it themselves. I actually did manage to survive and make a modest profit, not because I was smarter than my competitors, not because I had a better location (we had a C-location), not because I had better products (everyone basically had the same products), and not because we delivered a better shopping experience, but because I worked like a maniac for nearly twenty years. Often putting in fourteen-hour days, six to seven days a week.

Then in 1995, I received an invitation from a fellow menswear retailer and good friend of mine who lives in Philadelphia to join him and attend a one-day success seminar featuring many of the top speakers in the country. That's when I heard Dan Kennedy speak for the first time and that's when I realized that someone was finally handing me the combination to the lock that opened up the secrets to running a profitable business.

I immediately applied several of Dan's strategies to my business which produced sales and profits that skyrocketed off of our charts. As you can imagine, I was hooked and immediately bought all the Dan Kennedy resources I could get my hands on, subscribed to his "No BS Marketing Newsletter," joined his membership program, and studied all of the other great direct response marketing gurus.

My business continued to flourish and soon other retailers began hearing about me and asking me about my secrets. In 1998, at Dan Kennedy's urging, I assembled BGS Marketing System. Originally, I only offered it to menswear retailers, but the word continued to spread and I updated it to work for retailers in all categories of business.

After a thirty-three-year career as a successful retailer, I created my own financial freedom and I eventually sold my business, focusing my full-time attention to helping other retailers and other entrepreneurs grow their businesses.

Business Today

At BGS Marketing, I have 3,737 members all over the world including US, Canada, Spain, Israel, Ireland, United Kingdom, and Australia. I consult with people over the phone and at live events throughout the year. I work with Rory Fatt who is a marketing guru to the restaurant industry and created Royalty Rewards which is the #1 loyalty program in the world that puts retail businesses, restaurants, as well as service businesses new customer acquisition and retention on autopilot.

I am able to spend a lot of time with my family, donate time and resources to charities that are important to me, take vacations all over the world, and work when I want. I love helping retailers and other small business owners make more money and create a business that supports the lifestyle they desire.

As a retailer you can:

- Control your own hours
- Set it up to support the lifestyle you desire
- Be a celebrity in your own community
- Surround yourself with good products and good people
- Enjoy the social aspect to it
- If you plan wisely, establish wealth and secure you and your family's future

Turning Points

- Realizing I was the marketer of my business vs. the seller of the products and services that my business provided.
- Realizing that the most productive time I spent was the time that I worked on my business vs. the time I spent working in my business.
- That the value that I deliver is far more important than any qualifications I have.
- Surrounding myself with people that had expertise and abilities that I did not have.
- Realizing that the definition of management was getting things done through others vs. me having to do things myself.
- Realizing that you "can't give away good." Every time I give some of my knowledge and experience away to others, the success they achieve gives me more satisfaction back than I could ever give away.
- That I could accomplish more than I ever dreamed of and that money is actually easy to make once I decided to take action on my

ideas. I could actually get and accomplish more in twelve months than I had in the previous twelve years.

The Phenomenon™ Applied

In 1997, I saw Dan was coming to speak at another big event in Baltimore. I invited him to lunch, and showed him the unusual advertising I was doing. He urged me to publish and sell my advertising and marketing to other retail store owners – and as a spare time side business with one employee it continues to produce over a million dollars a year. That led me to really dig into what we call the "information marketing business," which encompasses publishing, consulting, coaching, and seminars. Today, as President of Glazer-Kennedy Insider's Circle™ as well as my original company, BGS Marketing, I oversee publishing four newsletters, a catalogue, a web store with over thirty-three different "how-to" products, over 130,000 customers, seminars, and a nationwide organization of consultants with ninety-four local chapters where like minded business owners meet to study this kind of measurable and cost effective advertising.

My KEY PRINCIPALS that allowed me to trigger The Phenomenon™ ™ three times so far are:

- **I thought like an entrepreneur, not a businessman**. A business owner remains limited by his own narrow definitions and only tries to grow his income; an entrepreneur expands his income by connecting many opportunities.

- **I realized it was more about understanding direct marketing and not necessarily having the best product or service.** Most businesspeople incorrectly think success is most closely linked to having the best products or services or unique products or quality of service or – worst of all – hard work. They do not understand that the critical element is truly understanding direct marketing.

- **I triggered The Phenomenon™ with a marketing SYSTEM.**

The Next 12 Months

The challenge most retailers face is that they get too caught up in the details of operating their business. They allow their employees, vendors, and even their customers to consume all of their time instead of spending time working "on" their business. When you work "on" your business instead of ONLY "in" your business, you'll find it is the most profitable time of your entire day, week, or month. What I teach my members is to set aside at least two hours every week to ONLY work ON their business without any distractions. This is the time to work ON your merchandising, ON your customer experience, and most importantly ON your marketing.

Words of Wisdom

Two things. One, If I can borrow from a Jim Rohn quote: "Poor people have big TVs and rich people have big libraries." Obviously, Jim's message here is you need to invest in yourself. You took the first step by investing in The Phenomenon™ book, but now you need to take the next step and continue to invest in your education. I try to make that risk free for you with my special trial offer. All you have to do is go to www.bgsnoriskoffer.com, claim your FREE report entitled: "How to Simply & Easily Discover the Hidden Wealth Buried in your Retail Business!" Plus…you'll ALSO receive two priceless bonus gifts, I've mentioned. Go to the website and see for yourself.

* * *

Bill Glazer is the number one most celebrated marketing advisor specializing in the retail industry. He is best known for his outrageously effective direct mail and direct-response advertising, lab tested with his own two exceptionally successful Baltimore stores. He won the prestigious RAC Award at the 2002 Retail Advertising Conference; in the same year the Small Business Administration honored Bill as one of the top two business people of the year for the State of Maryland. In order to meet the needs of independent retailers, he worked with restaurant marketing guru, Rory Fatt, and created Royalty Rewards, a loyalty program that puts all of their marketing, including new guest acquisition, on autopilot. Perhaps the shining jewel of his accomplishments was when Dan Kennedy, the foremost marketing genius in the world, asked Bill to join him and deliver the latest marketing advice to their thousands of clients worldwide. When asked why he chose Bill he replied, "Bill is as astute and able marketer as I am and, frankly, a more organized businessperson than I am!" His personal interests include cycling, tennis, reading, travel, and philanthropy.

Are You Ready To Learn The Retail Business Building Marketing Secrets That Will Have You Making More In The Next 12 Months Than You Have In The Last 12 Years?

Get Your "FREE Special Report"
"How to Simply & Easily Discover the Hidden Wealth
Buried in your Retail Business!"

Plus....You'll ALSO receive two priceless BONUSES:

PRICLESS BONUS #1: When you request your FREE report online, you'll also be invited to join me and listen in on my next FREE Tele-Seminar entitled: ***"How The Most Successful Independent Retailers Actually Use Specific Killer Marketing Tactics"***

PRICLESS BONUS #2: A FREE article entitled: ***"How Outrageous Advertising Turns Ordinary Retail Stores into Super-Profitable Marketing Businesses."***

Simply go to www.bgsnoriskoffer.com or call 1-800-545-0414 and leave a message and someone will call you back within 48-hours.

How to Get $100,000...$300,000... Even $500,000 (or more) Worth of FREE Publicity

Discover How Any Entrepreneur or Business Owner Can Boost Sales by Getting Publicity in Newspapers, Magazines and on Radio and TV Shows Without Spending a Nickel on Advertising

Bill Harrison and Steve Harrison

Phenomenon™ Experience: We first experienced The Phenomenon™ when they were forced to move our business in a new direction after 9/11. We realized two things: (1) We'd been spending all our time promoting our clients and hadn't spent enough time promoting our own business, and, (2) We needed to shift our business from being almost completely a service business to selling our own expertise. We quickly reinvented the company and began offering seminars, training, and consulting – all designed to help entrepreneurs and authors get free publicity for what they're promoting. In just twelve months, our business went from the edge of extinction to being almost completely debt-free and more profitable than ever.

Phenomenon™ STATISTICS

2001 – Year begins with mounting bills and debt from post-9/11 slowdown. Begin marketing first publicity seminar, thus beginning transition from mostly service business to also teaching others how to get publicity. Move pays off big-time and over $100,000 in debt is paid off.

2004 – Introduce Free Advertising & Publicity Profit System and begin helping business owners get publicity.

2005 – Begin offering Quantum Leap Marketing Coaching Program to help others get publicity and make more from their expertise. Sales top $3 million for year.

Opportunities for Success

We teach entrepreneurs and authors how to increase their sales by leveraging their expertise for maximum influence and profit. One of the ways we do this is by teaching them how to get free publicity in newspapers, magazines, broadcast, and online media. Most people don't realize they have knowledge and expertise that is interesting and valuable to other people. You don't have to be the most knowledgeable or even the most successful person in your field to attract positive and profitable media attention, but you do need to know how to approach the media in the right way. We provide information and seminars that help self-promoters attract publicity easily and inexpensively.

The other way we serve business owners and authors is by showing them, when appropriate, how to package and promote what they know. We show them how to create and market books, audio and video programs, seminars, and coaching programs. The sky really is the limit when it comes to all the profitable ways to package and promote what you know. Whether we're talking about getting publicity for your existing business or creating a whole new business with a book and other things, it all starts by first realizing if you've been in your field for any real amount of time, you have information that others will want. The media will want to interview you. Others will gladly pay you for what you know in some form or other.

Getting Started

Not long ago, I had a painter over at my house to paint my daughter's bedroom. He asked me what I do, and I told him. As I was explaining how we help business owners increase their sales by getting free publicity, he interrupted me and said, "Gee, maybe I should get some publicity for my business." So, I showed him how to set things in motion. Two weeks later, he was written up with a full feature story in the local newspaper and was getting business as a result. The really amazing thing about what we teach is that you can start getting publicity right away – once you know what to do and how to do it. It's not uncommon for entrepreneurs and authors, who use what we teach, to get thirty or more publicity opportunities during the year, whether that's a radio interview, article, speaking engagement, or something else.

We've helped more than 12,000 entrepreneurs, authors, and self-promoters get free publicity. We have NEVER met someone who couldn't get publicity, at least at the local level or in their particular industry. Anyone who thinks they can't get publicity or doesn't deserve it is holding themselves back from a significant amount of success.

The Early Years

We both were entrepreneurial from a young age. In fact, one of our first businesses was a writing and photography business. We sold articles and photographs to the Gannett newspaper chain. These were usually about events taking place at our high school. It was our introduction to journalism. Bill also worked as a freelance photojournalist for *Newsweek* and *United Press International*. From that experience, we learned some key things.

The first is that people shouldn't be hesitant to try to get media attention because the media regularly needs fresh people to interview. When you have to do a story or a show every day or every week, you're constantly facing deadlines. You have to come up with something your readers will be interested in. If someone approaches you with an idea for something you can do – even if they have something to gain by your doing the story, you're glad to hear from them.

The second thing we learned is that it's always important to think of what the readers will get out of the story. In other words, you may be making good money buying and selling houses, but if you want a journalist to do a story about you in the newspaper, you need to answer one important question: why would his or her readers care? If you can show they can benefit in some way, like showing them how to buy a house for 30% less than market value, or how to make $60,000 or more in their spare time, great, but it's essential that there be a payoff to the journalists, readers, or audience.

After college, we were working out of our two-bedroom apartment trying to make ends meet.

Business Today

Instead of working out of a two-bedroom apartment, we now have 8,000 square feet of office space. We've got a great staff of ten full time people and twenty-two part-timers and freelancers. The days of tapping credit cards or credit lines to keep the business going are long gone.

We just celebrated our 20th year working together as brothers. Many people tell us that's the most impressive mark of success, and we'd agree. In all those years, there have only been two occasions when we almost killed each other!

Turning Points

The biggest turning point for us occurred when airplanes crashed into the World Trade Center on September 11th. All of a sudden everything stopped. The phone wasn't ringing and business plummeted. The whole country seemed paralyzed with fear and uncertainty. It wasn't long before we were struggling to carry our high overhead. We had to go back to tapping credit lines just to meet payroll. Bill and I went for a walk outside the office and began talking about the possibility of closing the business and going our separate ways. Those were dark days.

Money Making Strategies

I can give you examples of people who have made thousands of dollars from what we teach. I can also give you examples of people who have made millions of dollars from what we teach. It depends on a number of factors, but there is no limit to what you can achieve. For example, Kellene Bishop is a business owner who heard me speak at a conference about getting publicity. Her first thought was, "Why would the media be interested in little ole' me?" She's in the mortgage business and has a company called Beehive Commercial Lending. But she heard me say again and again, "You can have anything you want if you just position yourself to be famous." She accepted what I was saying – that anyone can get publicity. She realized she had some expertise to share so she started contacting media. Her goals were modest initially. She landed fifteen articles within the first year, and these were in her industry. One of those was a seven-page feature story in *Broker Magazine* where they put her on the cover. She generated over $150,000 in new business from this free publicity – and that's just the business she can track. Yesterday, she sent me

BILL HARRISON AND STEVE HARRISON

an e-mail. She wrote, *"By the way, if you want, you can now put that I've made millions – literally millions – by implementing your free publicity strategies."*

Now, to be fair, she's in a business where one deal can be worth a lot of money. But the fact is that publicity has an infinite upside with really no downside or significant upfront investment. Once you know how to get yourself in print and on the air, it's like having a blank check on someone else's account.

The Phenomenon™ Applied

I think The Phenomenon™ really begins when people start to realize there are so many more people who could be helped by what they know and do if they could only reach them. For so many years, we had a successful family business but we were so narrow in how we defined what we did and who we could help. If you just take some baby steps forward – even if you feel a bit uncomfortable initially – you'll soon discover that there are a lot of people at radio stations, TV stations, newspapers, and magazines who will be thrilled to know about you. You'll also discover that there are a lot of people who would like to buy your information packaged in some form or other and they'll pay you a lot more than you might have thought.

The Next 12 Months

Readers could add tens of thousands, maybe hundreds of thousands of dollars to their incomes and attract customers with a lot less effort. Instead of being a salesperson who has to pursue people, make cold calls, send out mailings, they can become known as an expert – someone people call for advice and, ultimately, buy from. People will feel excited, proud and privileged to be doing business with someone who is famous. And they'll be telling their friends about you.

Words of Wisdom

The best advice I can give is this: the most important way to make The Phenomenon™ happen for you is to simply get started. Jump in the pool. That's the best way to learn. Of course, it helps if you first get some coaching and follow proven models – those two things will really shorten your learning curve significantly. The key is to get started.

10 Steps to Success with Free Publicity Methods

Step 1: Realize what you know has value and makes you an "expert" in the eyes of the media. Most people undervalue their own expertise – don't make that mistake. You'll be surprised how what you take for granted is interesting and valuable to others. You don't have to have written a book, be #1 in your field or have received publicity in the past.

Step 2: Learn how to create a hook that will compel the media to interview you. You need to quickly show the media how writing about you – or putting you on their show – will interest their readers or listeners. (For tips on doing so, go to www.YourFreePublicityTrainingAudios.com)

Step 3: Learn how to write a killer one page-publicity pitch that will grab the media's interest. The media gets bombarded with press releases and other pitches from people who want free publicity. You've got to quickly tell them what's in it for them when they interview you and why you'll make for an interesting show/story.

Step 4: Send your press release and/or publicity pitch to the right person at the right media outlets. Whenever possible, send to a particular person and call to verify the spelling of their name and title.

Step 5: Consider getting some training on what to say and do when being interviewed to come across well and maximize your chances of getting business from the publicity.

Step 6: Leverage the publicity you get by displaying or mentioning the publicity on your website and other marketing materials. Order reprints of articles and put them in your office and/or send them out to.

Step 7: Send the media a thank you note for the interview.

Step 8: Contact the media who interviewed you and see if they'd like to have you again in the near future, or use you as a source for future stories. Consider sending your "A-list" of media contacts something at least once a month.

Step 9: Continue to send out more releases and/or publicity pitches so you'll get a steady stream of publicity and sales.

Step 10: Pursue other methods of getting free exposure we teach through teleseminars, public speaking, writing books, and joint venture marketing.

* * *

Bill and Steve Harrison are the dynamic duo who have led thousands to gain free publicity, skyrocket sales, and totally transform their businesses. Co-founders of www.FreePublicity.com and Bradley Communications Corp, the two brothers helped launch bestselling books including Chicken Soup for the Soul and Rich Dad Poor Dad. Since 1985, they've helped more than 12,000 entrepreneurs and authors get free publicity locally, nationally, and internationally including on such syndicated notables as Oprah, Today, Good Morning America, Larry King Live, CNN, Fox News, USA Today, Wall Street Journal, ABC's 20/20 and many more. They are publishers of Radio-TV Interview Report, the magazine known as "the bible of the industry," which television and radio producers use to find guests.

Are You Ready To Discover How To Gain A TON of FREE Publicity AND Start Making More In The Next 12 Months Than In the Last 12 Years?

Allow Us Send You…Not One…Not Two…But… THREE FREE GIFTS Worth $97.00!

FREE Gift#1
"10 Easy Ways to Get Free Publicity For Whatever You're Promoting … Locally, Nationally or Internationally"

This 30-minute audio reveals how anyone in any industry can gain tons of free publicity…quickly and easily.

FREE Gift#2
"How to Get Booked as a Guest on Radio and TV Shows"

Would you like to get free airtime to promote your book, product or business on radio/TV shows nationwide? That's what you get when you appear as a guest on one of the over 5,000 radio/TV programs nationwide that use guests.

FREE Gift#3
"Want to Write a Book? 7 Key Things
You Need to Know First"

Writing a book could change your life and business forever. Done properly it can be a phenomenal publicity and lead generation tool that might even make you rich and famous.

**Simply go to
www.YourFreePublicityTrainingAudios.com
to get access to these audios and on your
way to achieving The Phenomenon™ in your life!**

Business Owners Learn How to Go from Working 70 and 80 Hours a Week, to Working Only a Few Hours Per Week... Make More Money Than Ever

Ron Ipach

Phenomenon™ Experiences I've had several Phenomenon™ experiences over the past decade. My first experience came after purchasing and operating a mobile windshield repair franchise full time for several years, I was only making $13,000 per year. A series of events led me to a Success Seminar in Cincinnati in 1995 where I met Dan Kennedy. After applying Dan's marketing strategies to my windshield repair business, I quickly grew my business to where I was making $13,000 per MONTH within the next 12 months.

My second experience came when I packaged up all of the marketing materials and strategies that I used to grow my business and started selling that information. I quickly became a celebrity in that industry for my no-nonsense approach to making money in a difficult business. That business went from zero to $30,000 per month within the first 12 months.

Then in 1998, I wrote and designed a complete Marketing Success System specifically for the auto repair industry and have helped over 4352 shop owners all over the world create their own Phenomenon™ experiences. In 2005, I created a high-end coaching program for the auto repair industry and launched that business and sold $720,000 the very first day I offered it.

Phenomenon™ STATISTICS

1995 – Met Dan Kennedy at a Success Seminar and quickly applied his strategies to my business and it grew to making $13,000 per month - working only 35 hours per week.

1996 – Started CinRon Marketing Group and sold marketing information to the windshield repair business. That business grew to $30,000 per month within the first year.

1998 – CinRon Marketing Group started selling the "Auto Repair Marketing Success System" which quickly grew to serving over 4352 businesses all over the world.

2005 – Launched "Pinnacle Performers" with sales of $720,000 in only one day.

2007 – Created "The Lazy Man's Way to a Successful Life" which teaches owners how modify their business and personal lives to make more money while working less.

2008 – Launched the "Repair Shop Coach" and the high-end "Repair Shop Coach Elite" Mastermind groups and grew to over 145 members in just the first two months.

Opportunities

First off, I'm a lazy entrepreneur. I don't like spending time working, yet I understand that time is necessary in order to run a successful business. The problem for most entrepreneurs is that they never have enough time to get everything done – and still have time to spend with their families and to go out and enjoy life. Most find themselves a slave to their businesses.

I broke free of my shackles by learning how to delegate almost every aspect of my business and now only work a few hours every week. I find that my business is stronger and better than if I tried to keep doing everything on my own. I often sacrifice making more money, in favor of spending more time with my family and enjoying life. I keep reminding myself about what I heard Zig Ziglar say, "I never once sat at the deathbed of anyone that said 'I wish I spent more time at the office.'"

My other core business is helping auto repair shop owners attract and keep all the best customers that their shops can handle. I developed a complete "paint by numbers" marketing success system that not only teaches the core principles of marketing as they apply to the auto repair industry, but I also provide my clients with several dozen ready-to-use ads, letters, and campaigns that they can easily customize and put to use for their own shop.

Getting Started

Ever since I was in high school, I had that entrepreneurial itch to be my own boss. While there was safety in working for someone else, I knew that the way to create a great lifestyle was through owning my own business. I started small by failing at quite a few ventures – selling ads on book covers, multi-level marketing, you name it – I probably tried to make money at it. Each time I failed, it looked at it as one less failure that I'd have to endure on my way to success. While most others would have given up after only one or two failures, I knew that the odds were in my favor to win. I finally decided to buy a mobile windshield repair franchise in hopes that someone else would give me the ready-to-use tools that would eliminate my record of failure. I invested in the best training, the best tools, learned to do an outstanding job repairing windshields – and wound up making in my best year, $13,000. That is until I discovered Dan Kennedy and studied –and APPLIED – his marketing strategies in my business.

Business Today

I now have over 4,352 clients in the United States, Canada, England and Australia. My ready-made client newsletter, being used by auto repair shops, dentists, realtors, plumbers, chiropractors, and several other business categories, is delivered to over 350,000 homes all over the United States and Canada every single month.

I can always be seen running my kids to their sports practices and I rarely, if ever, miss their games. At least two nights a week I play softball – with guys half my age, and golf whenever the urge hits me. The spring and summer months are always action packed in that we spend most of our time boating, skiing, swimming, and hosting parties for our friends and family. The pace of colder months slows only a little while we vacation in warm destinations except for the times when we are snow skiing. I schedule my personal life first, then, whatever time is left over I spend on real work.

I now take vacations three weeks at a time, and rarely ever talk with my staff when I'm away. Because I have surrounded myself with people that specialize in the support they offer, I am able to break the bonds of business ownership and travel with my family to exciting destinations that most only read about.

Money Making Strategies

By far my most spectacular story is one in which an overworked single store owner went from paying his employees by taking cash advances on his credit cards and being tens of thousands of dollars in debt, to having 21 shops and sharing a multi-million dollar income stream, while working less than 20-hours per week – all in the span of only five years. I've helped many others experience their own Phenomenon™ by increasing their businesses 50%, 60%, even over 100% within a 12-month period.

While these amazing increases are certainly possible for many businesses, the average business can easily add $30,000 to their bottom line within the first 12 months if they implement at least a few of my marketing strategies. Even better, they can take lots of time off away from their shops if they implement my "lazy lifestyle" strategies.

The Phenomenon™ Applied

What I'm most proud of is that I've achieved so much and continue to grow financially without sacrificing time with my family. I've watched too many "rich" guys bury themselves in work – and for what? A bigger home that they never see? A better car that they only drive to and from the office in?

The Next 12 Months

You've heard about the 80/20 Rule right? Well in this case, the 80% represents the majority of business owners that struggle every single day in their businesses to get by. The 20% represents the minority of business owners that are truly successful. The problem is, most business owners focus on replicating the efforts of the 80%ers and therefore will always remain in the 80% group. The 20%ers go against the grain and do things differently. They learn from the other 20%ers and do what they do. In order to break free from the 80% group and experience The Phenomenon™ for yourself, you must change almost every aspect of what you are doing today. Change your focus towards marketing. Look for the experts in the business that are super successful and learn from them and copy everything that they do. Invest in your marketing education and join a Mastermind group. That is what the 20%ers do every day and what the 80%ers refuse to do or see as an unnecessary waste of time and money.

Words of Wisdom

Never let anyone that does not share your goals and dreams tell you what you can and can't do and never take advice on how to be successful from anyone that has not achieved success. While you are reaching for a hand to pull you up, you'll find that there are others wrapping their arms around you trying to hold you down (you might even find that voice in your head trying to do the same!). This is the most frustrating part to those of us that are trying to help folks achieve The Phenomenon™ in their lives. Break free and allow yourself to take a chance at success.

10 Steps to Success

STEP 1: Do something. Nothing happens until you take the first step.

STEP 2: Step away from your business. Don't go to your office for one week. Go to a library or rent a hotel room and eliminate all distractions while you create your plan for success.

STEP 3: Focus on direct-response marketing. Without customers, you don't have a business. Set aside all other aspects of running your business and only focus on marketing that gets an immediate response.

STEP 4: Market to your current customers first. This is the #1 most valuable group for you to market to. They already know you and trust you, plus you've already invested time and money to attract them to you. Don't allow your competitors to pay more attention to them than you do. By far the best strategy to accomplish this is with a monthly newsletter.

STEP 5: Never create marketing from scratch when a proven strategy can be copied. Unless you are an accomplished master marketer, never try and do this at home. Your best success will come from duplicating the successful efforts of other sharp marketers.

STEP 6: Duplicate the process exactly. When testing a new marketing strategy that you already know has been proven to be successful, it is important that you duplicate the strategy EXACTLY as it is.

STEP 7: Test small, track your results and then go big fast. Never assume that a marketing piece will be a home run. Test it small, track the results, and if you get good results, go big fast. Don't waste time. Slowly ramping up your marketing will only delay your success.

STEP 8: Embrace failure. Nothing is a surefire winner; you will FAIL! Don't let the failures slow you down. Each failure improves your odds of having success the next time out. **STEP 9: Join a Mastermind group**. Locking yourself in a room with several other successful business owners and professionals every month or so will give you not only the outside look that your business needs and challenge every aspect of your business, it will also give you the kick in the pants that you probably need to get going in the right direction.

STEP 10: Let others do all the work for you. There is not enough time in the day to do everything you need to do to run a successful business. Find capable companies, employees, and virtual assistants to handle everything for you. Once you do this, you can run your business from a beach in Tahiti!

* * *

Ron Ipach is the most successful business advisor to the independent auto repair industry with over 4352 clients. He has personally coached and mentored over 356 repair shop owners to help them improve not only their businesses, but also their personal lives. Ron is featured in Dan Kennedy's book, Ordinary People, Extraordinary Entrepreneurs and Success Coaches and creator of the "Auto Repair Marketing Success System" and the "Lazy Man's Way to a Successful Life" system, Ron's interests include softball, golf, watching his kids play sports, travel, and quiet time with his wife to whom he has been married for almost twenty years. They live with their two children in Ohio.

Special Offer

A FREE Special Report…
"The Lazy Man's Way to a Successful Life"
(a $49.97 value)

In this 12 page report I show you how I did it and how YOU TOO can apply my "Lazy Man's Way to a Successful Life" strategies in your own business and personal life. Many of my clients have literally transformed their lives with these strategies and now you have this free opportunity to see just how it's done.

To get your FREE video and special report, go to…
www.MyLazyWay.com

…or fax a copy of your business card or your letterhead to (513)779-4990. Make sure that your name and all of your contact information is included and legible.

Creating the Lifestyle of Your Dreams by Achieving Optimal Health and Fitness

Lloyd Irvin

 **Phenomenon™ Experiences:** In 2002, while down and facing bankruptcy, I was introduced to Dan Kennedy via recommendation from a top advisor to the martial arts industry and Dan Kennedy follower/client Stephen Oliver. Fast forward to 2006, by implementing MANY of Dan's (and others') strategies, I have now grown that business to over $1-Million a year. But I didn't stop there.

I had a second Phenomenon™ experience in 2003, after receiving an e-mail from Dan recommending Ken McCarthy's 'Internet System Seminar'. I immediately registered and went. Blending what I learned from Ken with direct-response strategies from Dan, I launched my first product online which brought in $180,000.00 the first day – and that product has since brought in close to $4-Million!!!

My most recent Phenomenon™ experience was when I created another multimillion dollar business out of thin air, in the real estate investing field, so that my wife could quit her job. Together we now have over 500 investors in our coaching program. And, of course, I'm helping them experience The Phenomenon™ too.

Phenomenon™ STATISTICS

1995 - Income, zero.

1996-2002 - $57,000.00 in credit card debt trying desperately to keep his martial arts business afloat.

2003 - merged Direct Response Marketing into his business and saw sales skyrocket to $300,000.00 income, became debt-free.

2004 -Introduced Information Marketing to his business, increased earnings to $2.5-Million.

Opportunities for Success

I teach people probably one of the most overlooked aspects of being success-ful! I teach people how to get in shape without having to go to the gym, lift weights or spend hours on weird contraptions. You see, no matter how much money you make, if you don't take care of your health, you won't be able to enjoy any of it. A lot of people will teach you how to make money and, yes, I do that also but the people that I work with I want them to be able to enjoy their wealth for a LONG time. I've created products to help people from all walks of life get into the absolute best shape of their life, and the best part of it all is, they can do it in the privacy of their own home. I've also created a GAME that is taking the world by storm, it's called "BodyLow." It's a dice game that you play that will get you in amazing shape. You can do it at home, while on vacation, on a business trip, etc. I have people all over the world playing the game getting into amazing shape.

Getting Started

I had a struggling martial arts school, that was making about $3,600 a month and I was about to go bankrupt. This was my only business and source of income so it was a very depressing time. I was trying to model other martial arts schools that had been around for a long time and at that time I equated longevity with success, boy was I wrong.

I got an e-mail from a guy named Stephen Oliver asking me if "I would like to make an extra $100,000 in my martial arts school this year?" He was selling a product for about $350 to teach martial arts school owners how to make their businesses more profitable, it was called "Extraordinary Market-ing." I tore into that product and started implementing the strategies imme-diately. The funny thing was that I was in Brazil at the time getting ready for the World Championships of Jiu Jitsu and I must admit that this course took my focus off of the tournament quite a bit.

I became a Dan Kennedy maniac, listening to, watching, and following everything that Dan said to do in my businesses. I purchased his books, his training courses, attended his seminars and joined his mastermind groups. I got an e-mail from him one day that urged me to attend a internet marketing seminar by a guy named Ken McCarthy. Of course I jumped on the opportunity to learn about how to make money online. Attending Ken McCarthy's System Seminar was hands down one of the best decisions that I've ever made in my life. I started merging the direct response marketing I was learning from Dan with the online strategies that I learned at the System Seminar and went on to build my own online business empire. I attended the System Seminar in 2003, then I started creating my own information products and the rest is history.

Business Today

Well, I now have several businesses. My martial arts school is doing over a million dollars a year. My internet and marketing company is a multi million dollar business now and it's all because of what I learned from my mentors... and by taking fast action.

Turning Points

The single biggest discovery that rings in my head 24 hours a day, 7 days a week is the fact that no matter how much money you have, you won't be able to enjoy it if you don't take care of your health. Most people overlook it until it's too late and something bad happens that forces you to take a good look at your life. Not me, I get it, taking care of your health is first and having a good level of fitness, to help prevent cardiovascular disease, high blood pressure, high cholesterol and so many other health problems that could be avoided by simply having a structured workout. That's why NHB strength training has done wonders for so many people around the world. It's a simple, quick and easy solution for people to get into great shape.

Money Making Strategies

Let me first talk about the tens of thousands of people that I've helped with my World Class Fitness products because what people are achieving with their health far outweighs the money. Remember...if you don't have your health you won't be around to spend and have fun with all that money. The great part about what I offer is that it can help people from any walk of life, male or female... it doesn't matter. One of my students who was about 80 pounds overweight and was extremely tired with his professional life finally decided to make a change. He started following my system and after losing all of his excess weight he got the energy to get involved in the internet marketing business, he now makes six figures working only part time.

The Phenomenon™ Applied

My understanding of The Phenomenon™ is simple to the core, just like I focus on the core basics in the martial arts while most what to learn the latest greatest new technique. There are specific triggers that can trigger The Phenomenon™ for an individual. The Phenomenon™ clearly lays out what these triggers are. The "3 percenters" will follow, apply and take action making sure that they are doing everything in there power to make sure these triggers are in their life. I simply do everything that The Phenomenon™ teaches. I don't deviate, even if I don't feel like doing something, I do it, because I've made a promise to myself that I don't want to be in the 97% group.

The Next 12 Months

In the next 12 months a person could completely alter their life and their lifestyle. Some people will be able to make a million dollars, others may not move as fast as others and only make an additional six figure income, many people can fire their boss, but it's completely up to the individual and how fast they make sure that the triggers are working for them to experience The Phenomenon™. But most importantly a person can change their health and fitness level so that they can enjoy all of the wealth that they create.

10 Steps to Phenomenal Health and Fitness

Step 1: The most important step is to **decide** that you want to get into shape, that you understand that being in shape is very important to aligning yourself to live a healthy and wealthy life.

Step 2: Next is to sit down with your schedule and decide what type of **time commitment** you are willing to make in order to get in shape.

Step 3: Now focus on the activities you like (and dislike) so we can determine what your plan of action should be.

Step 4: Commit to having fun. You must make sure that the activity you choose is something that you enjoy. If your workout isn't fun, then the chance of sticking to it is slim to none.

Step 5: Before you start **take your body measurements, weight, body fat, etc**. One of the easiest ways to stick to your workout is for you to start seeing the results. There is nothing better then seeing inches melt off of your waist line, the number on the scale getting lower and lower each time you check your weight, it's very motivating.

Step 6: You have to decide if you are going to add an eating component to your new workout program. The way this works is depending on the type of workout that you do. No matter what you are doing in your life, you have two basic ways to start losing weight or getting into shape. You can increase your workout load and start seeing results or you can start eating better and start seeing results. In reality, you'll see the quickest and most dramatic results if you do both.

Step 7: Now it's time to **select a workout program**. Like I said earlier this is very important since it's what you are going to be doing to reach your goals and start living a healthy and wealthy life.

Step 8: It's time to get your workout clothes, if you don't have any you'll need some comfortable clothing. I prefer shorts, T-shirt and tennis shoes, my wife loves sweat pants, tennis shoes and a halter top. Whatever you choose just make sure that it's comfortable.

Step 9: It's now time to **pick a start date**. You have to pre-plan on your exact start date and how to determine how often you are going to workout. In the very beginning you have to be careful because you are all excited and may want to go overboard with working out. This is a costly mistake. It could force you into an early burn out, or worse, injury. I recommend that you start off with only 2-3 days a week at the max.

Step 10: Stick to your plan, your workout schedule and NEVER break it unless it's an emergency. You must put your health as a priority, just like people put so many other things that won't pay off like taking care of your body.

* * *

Lloyd Irvin owns Emory Marketing Systems, Emory Enterprises, Emory Realty, Emory Automotive, Maryland Real Estate Secrets, Lloyd Irvin's Mixed, Martial Arts Academy, World Class Training Secrets. Most known for 2005 Brazilian Jiu Jitsu World Champion, Lloyd is also 2 time National Judo Champion, 2 Time National Sombo Champion. Author of No Holds Barred Strength Training, How To Develop Killer Abs In Just 3 Minutes A Day and Bodyweight Conditioning For The Average Joe, Lloyd's personal interests include Gracie Jiu Jitsu, Thai Boxing, and Ultimate Fighting. He and his wife Vicki have one son, Lloyd Irvin III. They live in Prince Georges, Maryland

Are You Ready To Learn My Secrets To Getting In Peak Physical Condition So That You TOO Can Achieve More In The Next 12 Months Than You Have In The Last 12 Years?

Get Your "FREE Special Report"

"NO WEIGHTS, NO PROBLEM"
(a $39.97 value)

Truth is, you don't need anything fancy to get into the best shape of your life. Let me show you my easy system and the secrets that hundreds have used to transform their bodies and achieve more than they ever dreamed possible.

PLUS....I'm Going To Throw In ONE MORE Incredible FREE Bonus Report

"Discover the Secrets To How Being Healthy, Can Also Make You Wealthy" (a $29.97 value)

In this eye-opening report you will discover:

- How To Get Into The Best Shape Of Your Life In Only Minutes A Day
- How You Can Build Multiple Streams Of Income While Getting In Shape

- Discover Why You Can Lose All Of Your Wealth If You Don't Take Charge Of Your Fitness
- 3 Secrets Doctors Never Tell You About Your Health And Your Banker Doesn't Tell You About Your Wealth
- And much…much…more….

**Simply go to
www.LloydIrvinWarpSpeed.com
To get both of your FREE gifts worth $69.94
and get on your way to optimal fitness and the
lifestyle you truly desire!**

How Anyone from Any Background Can Quickly and Easily Learn a Profitable Skill or Trade and Rapidly Build Their Very Own Highly Profitable Business... All in 12 Months or Less

Gene Kelly

Phenomenon™ Experience: In 1987, I was the owner of a small manufacturing company that was on the verge of bankruptcy. It was in this desperate moment that I acted on an idea I had to make an "information kit" for a product that I had successfully built as a hobbyist. I placed a classified ad in a trade magazine and in just a couple of weeks experienced the "kitchen table, mail order thrill" of a post office box literally crammed full with eighty orders. That was my first Phenomenon™ experience; it saved my business and that product earned me over $1,000,000.

My second Phenomenon™ experience was just five years later in 1992 when I developed an accelerated process for teaching advanced electronic security techniques to hundreds of security professionals worldwide through an instructional video series. This skyrocketed me to the top of that industry.

In 1997, the third Phenomenon™ experience was in creating the Accelerated Training Institute. Based on feedback, I found that people wanted "how-to" information and that if provided it to them step-by-step on video, they would buy it. I have since educated thousands of students over the last ten years and currently generate over $3.1 million dollars a year.

I am currently experiencing another Phenomenon™ as I simultaneously launch a new book, a new online trade school, a coaching program for business owners and development of a new series of Priority-1 ™ tools for individuals and businesses to use to get more done faster, **www.AtiTradeSchools.com.**

While at the same time, expanding my continuity membership program that currently brings in over $52,000 a month in reoccurring revenue by growing it 250% in the next twelve months.

Phenomenon™ STATISTICS

1987 – Created first info-marketing product, which brought in over $8,700 in the very first month. This one product went on to make over $1,000,000.

1997 – Launched Accelerated Training Institute, currently Generates over $3.1 Million dollars a year.

2007 – Continuing to build and add new streams of income, including my continuity membership program that is currently bringing in over $52,000 a month in reoccurring revenue.

Getting Started

The traditional route to learning a skill or trade is to go to a campus-based trade school for a couple of years and spend tens of thousands of dollars, plus living expenses and lost wages to get a certificate or to become an "apprentice" for several years at a low wage. In either case, these programs usually do not encourage rapid advancement or speed and are based on the nineteenth century industrial age thinking that number of hours "butt-in-seat" somehow equals some level of competency. In fact, many of these programs are designed to hold gifted people back and make them "pay their dues." They really are a disguised series of obstacles intended to provide low cost labor that benefits and protects "journeymen" who have been in the system long enough to get seniority, but not necessarily competency.

Through the Accelerated Training Institute's use of video instruction any individual can learn at whatever speed they are comfortable, and not be held back by antiquated teaching methods. They can start and finish a course having learned a skill or trade and can go to work in as little as ninety days.

The Early Years

I started in the mail order business years ago out of desperation. I had a small manufacturing company and a major customer went bankrupt, stiffing us for a lot of money. We were desperate but I had an idea for a template kit that I myself wanted but couldn't find. I placed a classified ad and experienced the thrill of a finding a mail box literally crammed with orders.

Things really accelerated for me when I joined the Glazer-Kennedy Insider's Circle a couple of years ago, started attending the Info Summit, Super Conference and every other seminar that was offered. Plus, I was fortunate enough to have been selected to join both Bill and Dan's VIP coaching groups. I can't believe how much I have learned through those experiences. As a result of just one idea, I have now added continuity to my hobby gunsmithing courses that has resulted in an additional $50,000 plus in monthly income.

We started just a year ago and already have over 1,700 paying members generating $51,000 a month in recurring income, and we are on target to grow to 3,000 members and $90,000 a month by the end of this year. That's over a million dollars a year in recurring revenue and we are just getting started.

Business Today

Well, I'm a long way from my near bankruptcy days! I now have a net worth in excess of five million dollars, live very comfortably in the Napa Valley, and travel with my family on vacations several times a year. My son is in private school. Money is set aside for his education. I have over $1,000,000 in my retirement accounts. I own several houses and commercial real estate. My businesses are valuable and saleable assets. I drive what I want and live where I want and take vacations when I want. Life is good. God has blessed me.

Money Making Strategies

It of course varies greatly depending on the skill or trade that people choose to learn and then most importantly what they do with it. To begin with, people are primarily achieving lifestyle choices (the ability to work for themselves, or working in a trade that they want to do or that is higher paying or using these courses as a stepping stone to other things). The ones that really are successful financially in life are the ones who take what they have learned and leveraged it into owning a profitable business. These individuals often learn several different, but complementary, trade skills and also acquire business knowledge that enables them to grow their businesses and thrive. I have had students that were absolutely destitute that literally had to beg and borrow the money to get training they needed, that are now operating successful businesses. The results each person will get are directly linked to speed and quality of instruction in a chosen profession and their individual desire and drive to be successful.

The Phenomenon™ Applied

By being very clear about knowing what you want to accomplish, selecting the steps, by taking massive action, while enrolling others to also take massive action that benefits them as well as you. This truly is how you can achieve The Phenomenon™.

Let me break this down to the ridiculously simple for you…

1. Within the next twelve months a person could decide what they want out of life and start developing the plan to get there. For example: How much money do they want to make? The choices will certainly be different if they want to make $200,000 a year verses making $10 an hour. Where do they want to live? Why remain living in an area you don't like or one where it isn't conducive to achieving your goals? Decide how you want to spend your time. Create a firm, clear list of measurable Goals.

2. Commit to achieving the goals within a tight but believable timeline (believable to you, others don't matter) that will stretch you emotionally, physically, and financially.

3. Hunt down and purchase the education that you need to achieve the goal. If the goal is to own your own business, learn the trade skills required as fast as you possibly can (there are no awards for slow). Even though many organizations and schools will tell you that you need to spend X amount of time "served" to become proficient at something. That's simply B.S.

4. IF you strongly DESIRE to do so, start or buy a business. If you read the book *The Millionaire Next Door*, you will find that more people become rich through owning businesses than through any other method.

5. Learn everything you can about owning and operating a business. You must be willing to pay for high quality and timely information. While you can often get a great deal of information for free, that's often what its worth. Find the people who have been successful and learn as much as you can from them.

6. Fail forward fast! What I mean is you will often do everything right or almost right, missing a few key ingredients and still fail. So what? Pick yourself and keep moving forward. If you are moving forward quickly the "failure" is only a brief learning experience that will drive you on to success.

7. Then, after you have first invested in yourself, by purchasing speed through Accelerated Education, then from the fruits of your business or job, consistently take a fixed percentage or significant dollar amount every month and invest it in other opportunities such as real estate, stocks or businesses. Properly invested this will, over time, make you rich. Possibly VERY rich!

Words of Wisdom

Start now! Even when, or especially when, you are NOT ready, because if you wait until you are ready, you NEVER will be. Once you have set your goals, have quickly created and clarified your ideas as best you can with the information you currently have, do what Dan Kennedy often refers to as "Creating a Train Wreck." Move forward quickly and some things will become a bit of a mess to be sorted out, but the pure volume of activity driven in a focused, targeted direction, will often carry you onward toward success.

9 Steps to Success: The Tradesman to Millionaire System

STEP 1: Decide upon the end results you would like to achieve as you understand it now. What do your want your life to look like? Do you want a great job or career? Or do you want to be a business owner or possibly an investor? Try and be very clear with exact target numbers. For example, it is far more actionable to say: "I want to Make $250,000 a year," then to say: "I want to make a lot of money and have a million dollars."

STEP 2: Understand how important a factor SPEED learning a skill or trade is to your long-term success. Successful people don't wait to become rich. They learn a skill or develop an exclusive idea or product and leverage it quickly into a business or opportunity, which accelerates them past the rest of the pack, multiplying their returns on investment and quickly moves them toward their goals.

STEP 3: Appreciate the cost of time and its effect on opportunity. To fully understand this concept you need to also understand the power of time and compounding interest. A $100,000 invested today at 10% interest, re-investing the returns, would in thirty years be worth $1,983,740. But even faster growth can occur.

STEP 4: Select a path and get started now. For me the path was a campus based trade school. Although there was a lot of wasted time, thus taking far longer to go through that program then it currently takes to learn a trade with the Accelerated Training Institute (www.AtiTradeSchools.com).

STEP 5: Invest in yourself. Author, motivational speaker, coach and consultant Jim Rohn coined the phrase, "Rich people have big libraries, poor people have big TV's." This is a great visual and I have personally found it to be true with both the rich and the poor people that I have interacted with. Do you have a big library?

STEP 6: Move beyond being just an employee to becoming a business owner or investor. This advice is NOT for everyone. The path can be difficult and disastrous. You have to choose within yourself to make the necessary sacrifices to succeed in these areas.

STEP 7: Refuse to let others hold you back. There are lots of naysayers that just want to hold you back. "Why do you want to learn that?" they'll ask. "You're going to do what?" they'll say. But when you hear them this is what you need to do; first consider the source.

STEP 8: Wealth attraction techniques. There are reasons that money moves from one person or group to another. These techniques require studying and implementation, but they can be acquired just like any other skill.

STEP 9: Move from success to significances. As you create wealth and success in your life, tithe or give back a portion of it to acknowledge the blessings you have received.

* * *

Gene "Machine Gun" Kelly is the man who has shown thousands of regular folks how to quickly and easily learn a trade, build an incredible business, and become The Millionaire Next Door. He is the author of The College Myth: Why YOU Should NOT Go to College If You Want to Be Rich and Personal Protection & Security for the Very Affluent. He is founder and president of the Accelerated Training Institute, which has trained thousands of individuals in specialized trade skills. Gene has created the first Continuity Program in the hobby marketplace for "Firearm Enthusiasts," currently with several thousand members. He also teaches business owners how to excel and has recently developed Priority-1™ Software, a brand new strategic decision making tool that helps organize goals and projects, providing speed through clarity of action. Gene is one of the most recognized security experts in America, often interviewed and featured on television, radio and in print. He has worked on four continents training individuals and government agencies in security-related issues. He was the Glazer-Kennedy Info Marketer of the Year Runner-Up in 2006 and was also featured in the Information Marketing Association's magazine "Insiders' Journal" in January 2007. Gene dedicates much of his time and heart to Younglife, a non-denominational Christian youth outreach. He enjoys world travel and adventure, as well as shooting sports and hunting.

Are You Ready To Learn How To Put An End To Your Career and Money Worries, Quickly and Easily Learn a New and Highly Profitable Trade That Will Allow You To Achieve The Phenomenon™ In Your Life?

Allow Me To Send You...NOT ONE...but...
TWO FREE GIFTS!

Gene's Amazing Go-to-the-Head-of-the-Class Gift #1:
"A FREE Career and Job Profile Guide"

See what the hottest careers are that you can Learn FAST. Regardless of what you are doing right now, where you live or what type of education you have, this guide will show you many careers that you can easily learn in record speed so that you can create the type of income and life you have been dreaming of. No hype, incredible info and GUARANTEED results! You simply can't beat that!

Go to www.TheCollegeMyth.com for this eye opening FREE Career and Job Guide.

Gene's Amazing Go-to-the-Head-of-the-Class Gift #2: "My Speed System for Starting and Building a Business"

If you want to save YEARS of learning how to start and succeed in business then allow me to share with you my proven system, secrets and techniques that have led hundreds to build fast, new and highly profitable careers.

Go to www.AtiTradeSchools.com and sign up under the "Build a Successful Business Now" page for access to FREE special reports and on-going information that will help you achieve more in next 12 months than the last 12 years.

So, if you're ready to put an end to your career and money frustrations and start livin' life as it should be…happy, profitable and satisfied…then DON'T MISS THIS CHANCE. It'll take you less than 30 seconds…but those 30 seconds will change your life!

Found: Your Missing Phenomenon™ Link; Discover Ryan Lee's 21-Day Secret System for Achieving Superior Health and a Phenomenal Lifestyle

Ryan Lee

Phenomenon™ Experiences: I first experience The Phenomenon™ when I went from a physical education teacher in the Bronx to international fitness guru and Internet millionaire entrepreneur. In just 24 months I skyrocketed my income from six figures a year to over six figures a month.

Phenomenon™ STATISTICS

September 2001 – Started first paid membership site while working as a PE teacher. In the first month, earned over $5,000 (in addition to teaching income).

June 2002 – Even though he was earning a steady $5k-6k per month part-time while still teaching, Ryan left his full-time job as a PE teacher to dedicate all of his attention to his booming, new Internet business.

September 2002 – Just 3 months later Ryan was earning over $12,000 per month online.
Just 24 months later he was earning up to six figures per month and enjoying life like never before!

Opportunities for Success

I teach people how to reach the highest levels of achievement in their lives, both physically and financially. I provide coaching programs (delivered via monthly newsletter and audio CDs), membership websites, live events, teleseminars, and home study courses.

All of my programs show people, step-by-step, how to truly live the life of their dreams. My information is extremely practical and all "how to" information. There's no theory, just real-world applicable strategies to get the best out of your life. For example, I don't just tell someone to "exercise for 20 minutes a day," I give them actual workouts to do including the exercises, sets, reps and rest periods. I also teach people exactly how to create a fortune online and have complete financial freedom. Heck, if a PE teacher from the Bronx with zero computer skills and no marketing degree can do it, I can teach anyone how to copy my success.

Getting Started

The first step is to make your health a priority in your life, not just an after-thought. If you are only looking for a temporary fix or want to drop a few pounds for a wedding or class reunion, then you'll be on the yo-yo diets forever. When you commit to taking control of your health and fitness it directly affects your financial status. First, there are the physical improvements: more energy and stamina (so you can get more done), less sick days... the benefits go on and on.

Business Today

I now own over 50 different membership sites and have over 150,000 people on my e-mail list. I also have a lot of information products such as books, DVDs, CDs, software programs, and e-books. I run some live workshops, seminars and teleseminars, too. Recently, I launched a nutritional supplement business called Prograde Nutrition.

I have a small office outside of the home and a home office. No matter what, I'm always home for dinner with my family. And since I have wireless broadband on my laptop, I often work in different places just to change up the day. One day it might be a bookstore or another day I will do work by the pool. Now I am focusing on my new book and company, *The Millionaire Workout*. After helping so many people get into the best shape of their lives (both physically and financially) I decided to take all my strategies and put it into a format affordable for the masses – a book! I spent many months writing this book and I now write a monthly journal revealing my latest breakthroughs in both health and wealth. Now I get to help hundreds of thousands of people realize their dreams! I am truly blessed to earn the kind of income I do and have complete freedom.

Turning Points

1. If you want to reach the highest levels of success, you must be at peak physical condition. No exceptions!
2. You can get into phenomenal shape in less than ten minutes a day.
3. The more you invest in your education, the more you get back.
4. You must find people who are successful – and model them.

The Next Step

Before you begin my program (or any program for that matter) you must have a set of goals you want to accomplish. Your goals must be SMART.

Specific: Be as detailed and specific as you can with your goals. Instead of saying, "I want to be fit," you can say, "I want to lose 12 pounds of body fat in 12 months by working out for at least 12 minutes a day, five days a week."

The Phenomenon™ Applied

The Phenomenon™ to me is that moment when you really "get it." When you take specific steps to accelerate your success. It's when you take control of your own destiny; you stop making excuses and take immediate action. I've lived my life by these philosophies and it really works! While most people talk about success – I'm doing it (and living the life of my dreams!)

The Next 12 Months

You can dramatically improve your life. For example, you can lose 30 pounds and fit into the same size pants you used to wear when you were 20 years old. You can drop your cholesterol level 50 points. You can literally slow down the aging process. You can have more free time to spend time doing exactly what you want. You could build your own six-figure Internet empire based on your knowledge, skills or even your hobbies.

Words of Wisdom

Get rid of the negative influences in your life, set a specific measurable goal and take immediate, decisive action towards your goal.

10 Key Concepts of My Millionaire Workout System

STEP 1 GET FIT: You can get fit in as few as ten minutes a day! We've been told by experts you should workout at least 20-30 minutes a day, five days a week – and I'm here to tell you that is wrong. You can get a great, fat-burning, heart-pumping workout in ten minutes (or less).

STEP 2 GET FIT: The fat-burning zone is a big fat lie. You might have heard about "the fat-burning zone," where the slower you go the more fat you burn. The problem with this logic is while you might burn a greater percentage of fat; you actually burn more fat calories doing my type of exercises and workouts vs. traditional slow aerobic training.

STEP 3 GET FIT: You must eat more if you want to lose more weight. If you are trying to lose weight, the worst thing you can do is eat less frequently. The key is finding the right foods to eat and the correct frequency to turn your body into a fat-burning machine.

STEP 4 GET FIT: You do NOT need expensive exercise equipment. Stop wasting your money on expensive exercise equipment or gym memberships. In my book, *The Millionaire Workout*, the only equipment you need is your own bodyweight and a cheap set of dumbbells.

STEP 5 GET RICH: Leverage is key for wealth and happiness. The key to becoming wealthy and living a great life is leverage. You must learn to leverage your time and other people's skills.

STEP 6 GET RICH: Figure out your target market first. If you want to sell products online – you must first determine who you will sell to. There are valuable resources to help you find the right target market (like the SRDS); if you choose the wrong market, you are in big trouble.

STEP 7 GET RICH: It's not how much you make – it's how much you KEEP! If you want a less stressful life, consider keeping things simple and focus on the profits. And that might mean cutting out the less profitable ventures that take up a lot of time but drain your resources.

STEP 8 GET RICH: Recurring income is vital. Most people who create information products online focus on one day at a time and one sale at a time. If you want to build wealth, you need to create recurring revenue streams.

STEP 9 BE HAPPY: Go on a negativity detox. There are a lot of negative forces against you in this world. From friends who want to keep you down at their level to the slanted media, it's no wonder so many people feel like living a dream life is out of their reach. One place to start is with the radio. For the next few weeks, turn off the news programs and listen only to self-improvement audio programs.

STEP 10 BE HAPPY: Responsibility is the key. Here's the toughest pill to swallow. YOU are the one responsible for where you are today. If you are overweight or don't have enough money in your bank account, don't blame your parents or a bad boss – it is 100% your fault. This is a big step, but once you take responsibility for everything in your life, you'll be amazed how freeing it is and how your life begins to instantly change for the better.

* * *

Ryan Lee is the author of The Millionaire Workout and founder of the popular marketing web site www.ryanlee.com as well as the owner of dozens of web sites including ozworth.com, recurringrevenuereport.com, doneforyoublogs.com, strengthcoach.com, personaltraineru.com, and bodybot.com. He is the owner of a Nutritional Supplement Company, progradenutrition.com and software company www.fitnessgenerator.com. He is one of the world's leading Internet marketing coaches teaching people how to live the dotcom lifestyle. He enjoys spending time with his family, movies, traveling, and working out. He and his wife, Janet, have three children and live in New Canaan, Connecticut.

Are You Ready To Join the "New Rich" By Learning My Secrets That Will Have You Making More In The Next 12 Months Than You Have In The Last 12 Years?

Get Your "FREE $4,500 DVDs"

*Ryan is giving away free copies of his $4,500 per-person seminar DVDs
called "ePublishing-in-a-Box". This program teaches you, step-by-step,
how to build your own digital publishing empire, from scratch.
You'll learn every detail from setting up a blog to picking a topic
that sells to driving thousands of people to your site everyday.
No stone is left unturned and you get it all for free. All Ryan
asks is you pay s/h to cover his cost. That sounds fair, right?*

BUT Here's The Catch...

**Because he has a limited number of DVDs to give away,
they are expected to sell out I can ONLY give the first 75
People Who Go To www.ryanlee.com/12months these
FREE $4,500 DVDs. And once they're all gone...that's
all folks.**

BUT YOU MUST ACT FAST!
Simply go to www.ryanlee.com/12months

*Don't miss out on this incredible opportunity to learn my secrets
and experience The Phenomenon™ in your own life.*

Learn How Regular People Just Like You Are Bringing in an Extra $10,000, $25,000, Even $50,000 or More Per Month in Quick Turn Real Estate

Ron LeGrand

Phenomenon™ Experiences:

- Getting involved in real estate and changing my lifestyle
- Teaching what I know to lead me to be the best of the best
- Partnering with students on real estate deals

Phenomenon™ STATISTICS

1982 – I was a dead broke mechanic. One idea I picked up at a seminar led me to make $3,000 in 3 weeks using no money down or credit.

1984 – Built up a total of 276 units and over $1 Million in equity.

1987 – Four hundred houses later I'm the world's leading expert at quick turning houses.

1990 – Formed an information marketing company to package and sell live training events that led to over $200,000,000 in sales in future years.

2004 – Began teaching commercial real estate and began partnering with students, which made him more money in three years than he has made in his entire life combined.

Getting Started

Some come to us with a lot of experience, whom we have to rebuild and retrain, and others come who can barely spell real estate. We train doctors, lawyers, pilots, engineers, corporate execs, teachers, plumbers, nurses, housewives, and even the unemployed. All ages, areas, vocations and backgrounds.

All businesses are easy if the owner follows a system; all are hard if he or she doesn't. Real estate is no exception; you can make it hard or easy. Do it my way, it's easy and takes less time. The cost depends on how far and fast one wants to build a lifestyle. We have courses, live training, coaching and even come to you training. One can start with as little as $20 for my book *How to Be a Quick Turn Real Estate Millionaire*, in bookstores, or with live training and/or coaching, consisting of seven different events, and earn a master's degree, which costs $34,995, about the profit of one small, simple deal.

The Early Years

When I first got involved with real estate I was a dead broke auto mechanic trying to make enough money to make ends meet. Thirty-five years old, bankrupt and I didn't have a clue what I wanted to be when I grew up; but I knew it wasn't fixing cars in the hot Florida sun.

The year was 1982. I saw an ad that said something like, "Come learn how to buy real estate with no money or credit." It appealed to me because I had no money or credit. So, I attended the free seminar. The instructor got us all excited about real estate and showed us how people were buying real estate with no money down. Then he said, "If you pay $450 and attend our two-day training this weekend, we'll show you all the secrets." I wanted in but I had a problem, actually 450 of them.

But something compelled me to find a way to get the money and that's what I did. I borrowed it from two friends and showed up for the seminar. That decision changed my life, my family's life and their family's lives for generations to come, not to mention hundreds of thousands of my students and their descendants. That one small split second decision that could have gone either way made me millions of dollars since and spawned countless numbers of millionaires all over North America and other countries I can't even pronounce. That was my first Phenomenon™.

Business Today

Now, much of my time is spent in front of good people who are serious about getting rich and will do what it takes to become one of the three percent who can really say and prove they have achieved true wealth.

People constantly ask me why I continue to teach. It's hard for them to understand why a multimillionaire would take the time to work with those who aren't. My answer is simple really. First, make no mistakes about it, I get paid well for teaching. It's not a mercy mission and we're not a non-profit organization. Second, I have to do something with my time. Golf, fishing and diving get old quick. Making millionaires never gets old and I can't think of anything I'd rather do in my life. It's fun to be me and I love doing it. Besides, I've been married for over 42 years to one woman. Her name is Beverly and between the honey-do's and the nine grandchildren (three live on our estate) it's nice to get away once in awhile. Beverly says even though we've been married 42 years, if you take out my travel time, its closer to three.

Turning Points

I've had only a few breakthroughs, but they were big ones. The first is when I decided to ditch my job and take my life back. The second was when I started teaching what I had become good at. This opened up a whole new world of information marketing, which provided me a large income by doing what I love—teaching. But the biggest breakthrough came when I combined my real estate knowledge with my information marketing, and allowed my students to start sending me deals to partner.

Getting Started Today

It's ten times easier today than it was when I began. We have systems, technology, automation, and my twenty-seven-year track record one can follow like the yellow brick road and shave twenty years off the learning curve. Frankly, an idiot could make money in real estate today.

Getting Started

There are five steps to your success in our business or any other. These same steps apply regardless of what business you're in. Here they are:

1. Locate Prospects—without them you have no business.
2. Prescreen Prospects—there's a big difference between suspects and prospects. Prospects need to sell. Suspects want to sell. We can't buy

from suspects; in all businesses you must seek out the people who want to do business with you and whack the rest at lightning speed.

3. Construct and Present Offers—if you deal only with prospects, they'll make you the offer. There's nothing for you to construct. If you deal with suspects, any offer you construct won't work, and if it does, you won't like the results.

4. Follow Up—82% of all revenue in any business comes from the second through seventh contact with a prospect. After they have been prescreened, it pays big dividends to follow up with the handful of prospects you'll receive each month that are worthy of your time.

5. Close Quickly—the faster you get the money, the better you'll like the business, and the more business you can do. Selling houses is quick and easy, if you do it my way.

The Phenomenon™ Applied

The first thing is to get over the fact that real estate is some kind of mystical, complicated business that you have to be a genius at to succeed. It's not a hard business if you take a few simple basics and apply them to the market-place. Once you begin to see the wealth it creates, your commitment level will escalate. When that happens one can apply the same energy and enthusiasm generally wasted on worthless projects and achieve a quantum leap. If you want to make a lot of money, you must first put yourself in a position to do so. Real estate is the vehicle to do just that. Give it the same tender loving care you give your dog and it will set you up for life.

The Next 12 Months

You're worth what you set out to achieve. If you swap hours for dollars, that's your choice. You can think, or you can labor for those who think for you. You can make money or excuses. No one cares whether you're wildly succeed more than you, and the people you hang around would rather you fail. If you listen to the broke people who try to teach you to be rich, you'll get advice worth exactly what it cost. Nothing. Don't listen to morons. To earn more, you must learn more. It's not about working hard; it's about working smart. My credo that changed my life is: "The Less I Do, The More I Make®"

When you begin to spend your time doing the right things to make yourself rich and jettison all the worthless minutiae that sucks up every day of your life and focus on the few critical tasks you should, amazing things begin to happen and new worlds of opportunity appear. All people are self-made; only successful people admit it.

10 Steps To Success With My "Quick Turn" Real Estate

STEP 1: Decide this is the day you'll take your life back and make a commitment to spend a little time and money learning the basics of one of the oldest businesses in the world, real estate, from one of the oldest and best qualified teachers, Ron LeGrand.

STEP 2: Learn my simple system to implement the five steps to buy and sell houses with no money or credit anywhere in North America and beyond.

STEP 3: Begin to implement the simple steps starting with locating prospects using my time tested and proven low cost tools to flood you with more motivated sellers than you can serve.

STEP 4: Quickly prescreen out the majority, who are time wasters, with my auto pilot system, and work with a few who are ready to help you help them. This will take about 15 minutes a week and you won't be taking any inbound calls.

STEP 5: Go see two or three houses per week that have been prescreened and are ready to buy, and get a simple purchase agreement on the one or two you want that meet my criteria to buy without using your money or credit or making promises you can't keep.

STEP 6: Have your attorney do the paperwork and close in a few days.

STEP 7: Use one of my fast, step-by-step selling methods to move the house quickly and collect a big check within 30 days of the purchase.

STEP 8: Gain confidence, knowledge and cash profits. Begin utilizing more of my strategies, keep Quick-Turning some properties for cash income, become an investor retaining other properties to create wealth and continuing passive income streams.

STEP 9: Become a professional real estate entrepreneur just like me! Graduate to commercial properties, not just residential properties. Work cooperatively with other investors—my students network with each other, do deals with each other, even bring deals to me.

STEP 10: Become financially independent. Create steady, secure multiple streams of income to meet whatever your lifestyle needs may be. Secure your retirement by having your IRA, 401K and other pension funds buy and control profitable real estate for you, tax-free! And, get much greater wealth accumulation than leaving that money sleeping in low interest CD's!

* * *

Ron LeGrand is a residential and commercial real estate investor and restaurateur, as well as the principle of a seminar, training, and publishing organization working with thousands of new and experienced real estate investors. He is known for teaching unique opportunities in "quick-turn" real estate. The author of How To Be A Quick-Turn Real Estate Millionaire, he speaks over thirty times a year, including a number of programs with celebrity entrepreneurs like Donald Trump. He has personally bought and sold over 1,600 residential properties and is currently developing twenty commercial projects simultaneously. Ron's interests include oil projects, fishing resorts, and theme parks; he also enjoys fishing and diving. He lives in Jacksonville, Florida and owns a fishing lodge in Ketchikan, Alaska. His 42-year marriage to his wife, Beverly, has produced four children, nine grandchildren, and two great grandchildren.

This Book Is Making Millionaire$!
It's Your$ - FREE

Learn how a dirt poor auto mechanic accidentally discovered the simple secret of getting filthy rich in real estate without using his money or credit and you can too! Ron LeGrand has purchased over 1600 houses, $300,000,000 in commercial real estate, shared the podium with Donald Trump, Dr. Phil, Tony Robbins, Robert Kiyosaki, movie stars, presidents, sports heroes and business legends and has over 300,000 students across North America.

*He's just released a new CD called "***How to Make a Fortune in a Slow Real Estate Market***" and you can buy it for only $6.95 S&H and when* *you do, he'll throw in his book "How To Be A Quick Turn Real Estate Millionaire" worth $21.95* **ABSOLUTELY FREE***!*

This could be the most important $7 investment in your life. This guy really does make millionaires. He says it's not about working hard. Job slaves work hard, rich people work smart. "Anyone spending more than 10 hours a week buying and selling houses is doing it wrong."

"The Less I Do, The More I Make"®
—Ron Legrand

Order his CD and book and see how ordinary people are building extraordinary lifestyles almost overnight. They come from all professions, vocations, and age groups to learn the secrets of this millionaire maker.

Your cost is $6.95 S&H for the hot new CD. Ron will include his book at no extra cost and ship them to you right away! Procrastination could cost you a fortune.

Global Publishing Inc. VIP Services 1-888-840-8389 and www.RonsFreeGift.com

How to Start or Transform a Struggling eBay Business Into a No-Fail, Money Generating Machine
Andrew Lock

 **Phenomenon™ Experiences:** Like so many people, in the past I went through some very hard times. On more than one occasion I sold valuable personal possessions to meet the bills. My big breakthrough was discovering Dan Kennedy and his unconventional style of marketing. I applied the techniques I learned from Dan in my eBay business (by doing the opposite of what most people do on eBay). Things turned around very quickly, and within a short time I was literally making more money in twelve months than in the previous twelve years.

Today I'm happy to share that very same system with others, as I really believe that there's plenty of opportunities for many more people to profit from eBay - the world's largest and most popular e-commerce website! I also genuinely believe that eBay is one of the easiest ways to establish and run a new business.

Phenomenon™ STATISTICS

1999 – Started selling on eBay, struggled to make a profit.

2000 – Began making $1000 a month consistently on eBay, by reselling items from the Dollar Store.

2003 – Introduced to Dan Kennedy and immersed myself in his books/courses to learn REAL marketing that works.

2004 – My income from eBay doubled in the first 6 months, & quadrupled in the second 6 months.

Opportunities for Success

I have produced a replicable system for profiting from eBay (that's just a fancy way of saying you can copy it). Knowing that different people like to learn in different ways, I've developed numerous educational opportunities to suit your personal preference – printed manuals, audio CD's, DVD's, a members only website, instructional videos on screen and even live webinars. Regardless of the method however, I reveal the exact, step-by-step processes that I personally used to leverage eBay in unconventional and very powerful ways, and the information is constantly updated with all the latest tips, techniques and strategies.

Getting Started

It will be difficult not to sound biased here, but I really believe that eBay presents one of the easiest ways to make money right now compared with any other Internet business. Why? It overcomes the main challenges that online businesses have which I call the two T's – Technical and Traffic.

I'll explain…

Take the first one: Technical. Most people aren't technical and they find it daunting to build and maintain a website. Sure, there are templates and web-building software, but none of those solutions are ideal. To build a website properly and understand HTML—all that 'techy' stuff is a complex skill, so most people fall at the first hurdle.

The second aspect: Traffic, is equally important and just as challenging. Traffic is simply another way of saying getting visitors to a website. Anyone that's been around the world of selling on the Internet knows that the expression: "Build it and they will come" is completely untrue online. They won't come, because they don't know your website exists! That's why you hear so much talk about SEO (search engine optimization) and web traffic. It's the holy grail of the Internet. Everyone wants it and very few people have figured out how to get it.

The Early Years

I graduated from Winston Churchill School in Surrey, England in 1988 and for the next fourteen years I fumbled around with various business ideas, not having any real direction. Sure, I made some money on eBay, but like most sellers, I fell into the trap of thinking that eBay itself was the business. That was very shortsighted. Once I immersed myself in learning from Dan Kennedy things turned around rapidly.

Business Today

Doing something I love and being paid for it is the ultimate circumstance as far as I'm concerned. The fact that I'm being paid *more* for working *less* is the icing on the cake. Perhaps the biggest rewards are freedom of choice and not having to answer to a boss. I never did well working for someone else, but I've flourished with my own business.

Turning Points

The biggest breakthrough in my business education was learning not to be afraid of doing the opposite of what most people do. Actually, in many cases, that's a surefire recipe for success.

Within eBay, I made many significant discoveries that have literally revolutionized the way that eBay is used in my business, and those of my students.

Here are some big breakthroughs that I discovered about eBay:

1. eBay is not just a garage sale or a place to clear household junk. You can sell virtually anything on eBay, even services.

2. Most eBay sellers are going about it in the wrong way and they don't realize why it's not working. They just give up after a short space of time. Many stubbornly refuse to believe there's a better way.

3. **eBay is where the largest group of buyers are on the Internet.** In other words, people that visit eBay do so because they are ready to buy. That's a huge distinction compared to people searching say, Google. Most of those are not buyers, they are simply looking for free information. They are browsing, not buying.

4. Internet users spend far more time on eBay than any other e-commerce website, making it by far the most popular shopping destination on the Internet. Again, why would you want to ignore that huge mass of buyers ready to throw their dough at you, if you'd only give 'em the chance!

5. The belief that most people visit eBay to find the lowest price for an item is completely untrue. Stats from the independent research firm Nielsen/NetRatings show that to be near the bottom of the list of

reasons why people use eBay. Actually, *the number one reason people visit eBay is because of the availability of unique items.* If you can offer something unusual or unique, you can make a lot of money from eBay.

Words of Wisdom

Whether or not you've had any experience on eBay, the past is irrelevant. With the unique system I developed for eBay, you do not need to understand anything about eBay other than that it's an amazing opportunity.

Decide now that this will be a turning point in your life and be committed every day to furthering your goal. This guide will be of no use if you allow it to simply decorate a shelf. It has the power to change your life but only you can take that first step. I look forward to helping you succeed. Nothing will make me prouder than to hear your success story.

Here's What to Do Now

The easiest way to get started is to head on over to: **www.SendMyFreeGift**.com and request your FREE eBay Starter Pack (just pay a small amount towards the shipping to prove that you're serious rather than curious).

10 Steps to eBay Success:

STEP 1: Decide what business appeals to you and make a firm commitment to follow through with it. Dedicate time on a daily basis to do something to progress the business, even if it's just thirty minutes. Consistency is very important, you need to get into the habit.

STEP 2: Don't be distracted by other opportunities. Focus on one business, otherwise, you'll be pulled in many directions, your efforts will be watered down, and it'll take you longer to succeed.

STEP 3: Realize that there is not one best business for every person. Different things appeal to different people and what works for others may not work for you. There are many ways to experience The Phenomenon™. Be confident in knowing that it will work for you using eBay as the 'ready to go' platform.

STEP 4: Don't let your family or friends put you off or pressure you. Why would you listen to others who know less about a subject than you do, and let them influence you?

STEP 5: Don't read books about eBay from conventional sources. For the most part they are written by employees of publishing companies or inexperienced sellers who write books for their living. Not all books fall into this category, but be very wary of what you read.

STEP 6: Don't waste your time on the forums on eBay or elsewhere on the Internet. They'll suck your time and you'll be given bad advice from people who spend more time chatting about business than doing it!

STEP 7: Realize that beyond anything else, you are in the marketing business. You are selling something that other people want. You are not in the eBay business or the Internet business, or any other kind of business. You are in the marketing business. That's an important distinction that is lost with most people.

STEP 8: Meet with a local Mastermind group that discusses Dan Kennedy marketing, if possible. You'll reach The Phenomenon™ stage of your business much faster when you have other like-minded people helping you. Of course, you'll naturally want to help them too – the more you give, the more you'll receive.

STEP 9: Have an open mind. You'll almost certainly have to unlearn things you were taught in business school, college, university, and on the job. Embrace positive change; realize that you're moving forward much faster than before.

STEP 10: Be patient. It takes awhile to become an overnight success! The Phenomenon™ will happen without warning, and often at a time when you feel like giving up. Your results will probably be sudden and dramatic; you won't be able to stop it, the snowball effect will kick in.

* * *

Andrew Lock has shown thousands of eBay hopefuls how to build wildly successful businesses in the highly competitive online marketplace. He is an internationally recognized expert on how to use eBay in unconventional ways and is also considered a leading professional seminar speaker. Andrew has become known as the renegade auction seller and his company, Andrew Lock Consulting (www.HelpMyBusiness.com), helps entrepreneurs and small businesses profit from eBay by using it as a powerful lead generation system.

Are You Ready To Learn How To Start and EXPLODE Your eBay Business, BLOW Your Competition Out Of The Water and Get Moving Down The Path That Will Have You Making More In The Next 12 Months Than You Have In The Last 12 Years?

Great, Now Allow Me To Send You A FREE GIFT Worth $594.39 that will Show You How to Build Traffic, Generate Tons of Leads and Make You More Money Than You Ever Dreamed Possible...all on eBay!

BUT YOU MUST ACT QUICKLY!

I really want you to discover and experience my genuinely radical, renegade way of working eBay that will open your eyes and leave you wondering why this information was hidden from you until now. Intrigued? Well, you had better get a move on before they are all gone...

Hundreds of thousands of people from all over the world are going to be watching The Phenomenon™ and seeking to experience the same life-changing experience in their own life and business. Problem is...I only have 250 of these $594.39 FREE GIFT packages to give out (my accountant only wanted me to give 50 away ...so he still isn't speaking to me!)

Go right now to www.sendthefreegift.com, and you can get all the details of this VERY Special FREE Gift Opportunity.

Here's a snapshot of what you will receive:

"The Ultimate eBay Resource Toolkit" **($199.00 value)**

Enjoy "The Renegade Auction Seller Insider" Printed News-letter for One Month **($40 value)**

Exclusive 'audio interview of the month' CD **($59 value)**

You'll also receive 3 ADDITIONAL CDs of some of my most revealing interviews ever

($275.48 value)

Attention Dentists, Professionals and Entrepreneurs... Breathe New Life into Your Practice and Business.

Discover How You Too Can Learn My Proven Secret to Building a Wildly Successful Practice or Business, and START seeing a 30%, 50%, even 65% Increase in Production ALL in 12 Months or Less!

Dr. Charles Martin

Phenomenon™ Experience: I have experienced The Phenomenon™ several times throughout the last six years. First, in 2002 I went from a six dentist, thirty-five-member-practice producing $2.4 million annually to today practicing alone (with only six on staff) and still producing $2.4 million. The increase in profit and even time off with a decrease in stress levels has been a Phenomenon™. Since then, I have been starting new businesses and teaching others how to achieve the same levels of success.

Phenomenon™ STATISTICS

2001 – Introduced direct marketing and business building techniques to practice and increased earnings to 2 million.

2004 – Started mentoring and coaching other dentists, adding a high six figure income while simultaneously growing the practice.

2006-2007 – Started new businesses that went from zero to over one million in the first year of existence.

Opportunities for Success

I teach people who sell their time for money how to break the chains of time and the limits on making money imposed by charging by the hour. If one has experienced the fact that time is money, what I teach is probably appropriate. This encompasses quite a few people. It includes all members of the professions like dentists, chiropractors, lawyers, physicians, architects and accountants. It includes other professions, too. It includes consultants of all types, entrepreneurs, and small business owners. Really anyone in a service industry who is exchanging their time, care, skill, and judgment for money needs help as a Timeseller to break the chains that really prevent him or her from achieving all of the success that rightfully should be theirs.

Getting Started

The rigors of gaining a professional education and then in succeeding in one's own practice or business are not for the faint of heart. It's rough. The average professional practice takes ten years and hundreds of thousands of dollars to reach a respectable income level. For the small businessman or entrepreneur this process on average takes even longer. What's worse? The ninety-six percent failure rate. That's right, a ninety-six percent failure rate over a ten-year period. That is the chance of success of a small business in the United States, according to the Small Business Administration.

The Phenomenon™ for Timesellers is about beating the system everyone else plays by – the system that makes them only as good as their competition. The Phenomenon™ for Timesellers is about achieving a whole new level of success. It does take some new thinking and it does take some hard work, but doing the right work makes the difference.

Business Today

It took me longer than I wanted, but today I still take my ten weeks vacation per year and now I have a seven-figure income. I still practice, run a number of other businesses and teach. I teach because I love to see the deserving who've earned the right to attain super success. I want my clients to become the people they've always wanted to be while building a big booming business or practice. Frankly, that gives me a thrill. Oh, I still work plenty hard but it's different now. I have the freedom to choose, the freedom to travel, the freedom to further my intellectual and humanitarian pursuits. It's more fun and more rewarding personally and professionally. I had this future in mind and I felt creative and now I'm helping others do the same.

Money Making Strategies

Honestly, you could make millions. It all depends on how closely you follow the systems. One client told me he saved $750,000 with just one idea. The great thing about not spending the money is it's instant net. Typically, a client will increase twenty-five percent in the first year of working with me and then continue to do so each year thereafter. I've had clients go up as much as 400 percent over a period of two years. Here's the kicker. Once the increase occurs, it just continues to go on and on and on. They don't revert back. Now, if you just tally up a $100,000 increase in a year, over ten years that's the first mil, but it wouldn't stop there. My work will allow them to retire with a smile on their face at the time of their choosing and the financial freedom to have the retirement they always wanted.

The Phenomenon™ Applied

The Phenomenon™ for me is about changing your way of thinking, changing your way of doing, and then operating by rules that I've set. I have enjoyed wild success and I can help you do the same thing. I've built myself up and with that I've built my own practice up. I've gone from six dentists doing $2.4 million to just me doing $2.4 million with ten weeks off. I think that would be pretty much a phenomenal result, but I'm going to share three principles with you that I've applied and there are more of these, believe me.

Principle number one, not all clients have the same value. The 80/20 Rule says that it's only twenty percent of your clients that give you eighty percent of your profit. But here's the second part of the 80/20 Rule: it's the twenty percent of the twenty percent that really give you your income. You see, it's that twenty percent of that twenty percent that give you as much as two-thirds of your income.

Principle number two, clients want to trust you, to be taken care of, and to be guided. It is your job to be that trusted advisor and to guide them into making the right choices. Yeah, that means you have to have integrity. Integrity doesn't have a price tag until you lose it.

Principle number three is value. As long as the value you deliver is equal to or greater than your fee or price that you charge then your clients, patrons or customers will gladly pay it. See, it really is all about value that you bring. It isn't that much about time. A big critical issue for the Timeseller wanting to explode his income is to understand he's delivering a customized service. It is one of eight different types of general businesses that is in America today and as a customized service you have to diagnose and deliver, literally manufacture, the product itself or the service.

The Next 12 Months

Readers could, indeed, experience far more in the next twelve months than in the past twelve years if they are willing to change their thinking, let nothing stop them, and choose the right coach who knows the path and has the tools to help him get there. It's important for the person wanting to experience The Phenomenon™ to make the decision to do it, to act on it, and then to follow through. If a person thinks The Phenomenon™ will occur just by showing up or continuing to do what he's always done without changing he's in the dark. It just isn't going to happen.

No, it is hard, but fruitful work that leads to lasting improvements. It's about doing the right work so you can have the success that you deserve. It's about getting more time and making more money. It's about having a business or practice based on your rules. It's about more freedom. It's about professional satisfaction and personal satisfaction, too. That's The Phenomenon™ and that's something a Timeseller can have.

Words of Wisdom

Never stop dreaming the big dream. It creates the energy and passion deep down where it really matters – in the gut. Picture what you really want to have and then decide to go get it. Remember, the universe listens and works on your side when you know where you are going and make strides forward with a positive attitude and conviction.

I look forward to talking with you, working with you and being the coach that helps move you from the limits of being a Timeseller into a whole new realm.

9 Steps to Success from Experiencepreneur™, Timeseller and Phenomenon™ Thought Leader

STEP 1: Decide what you want to have. This is first for a reason. Only a small percentage of people ever make this decision. First decide and then watch your world shift. It is magic.

STEP 2: What are you passionate about? What would you do for free if you had to? Since you are going to be doing this for a long time, wouldn't it make sense to enjoy what you do so thoroughly that it doesn't seem like work?

STEP 3: Design your business and life around your talent and what you want to have. The key here is what you will not do. Good design eliminates and accentuates. Figure out how you can do more of what you love and less of what you don't.

STEP 4: Find out who's already been very successful in your field, area of talent, or adjacent one. Find out what they did and learn from their actions. Caution: If you do what the average are doing, you'll get the same average results.

STEP 5: Create your business or practice so you can charge higher prices and have your clients/customers/patients love it. (This is where I excel, in particular, in designing and managing the mindset, strategy, positioning, PR, marketing, sales, and the experiences you make for your clients. This is called Experiencepreneuring ™.)

STEP 6: Decide what you have more of: time or money. Then apply most abundant resource at multiple points that will forward your strategy toward what you want to have.

STEP 7: Assemble a group of likeminded people to aid you in achieving your perfect business and lifestyle. These will include:

Your Coach: Someone who has gone where you want to go and has a record of helping others get there, too. Find someone that resonates within you – how you think, what you feel and what you value.

Your Mastermind Group: The sheer synergy and energy of a group of forward-thinking, smart people thinking and working on your behalf and you on their behalf creates logarithmic leaps ahead.

STEP 8: Design your milestones that lead to your perfect business or lifestyle. I say perfect, while understanding perfect just doesn't exist. Still, the only way to get better is to work towards excellence, making progress everyday. The joy comes from learning, the journey of experiences and relationships and the mastery of the process.

STEP 9: Measure as you go; that which you can measure you can manage. Simply counting anything leads to near instant improvement.

Your Bonus Step: Celebrate your successes, but don't dwell on them or get stuck in the success. Take some time to reflect on what worked and why. Keep doing what is working while continuing to look for better, more effective ways.

* * *

Dr. Charles Martin, the man who has led thousands of dentists and other professionals to achieve amazing marketing results with his done-for-you systems and coaching programs operates a single doctor practice with six staff producing $2.4 million in profits. He is the author of chapters in two of Dan Kennedy's books, "The Dentist Guide to Nearly Everything," "Timesellers: How to Escape the Trap of Charging by the Hour," and "How to Charge More and Have your Clients Love It."

Are You Ready To Learn The Proven Strategies and Secrets That Will Have Your Practice And Business Making More In The Next 12 Months?

Allow Me To Send You…NOT ONE…NOT TWO but…
Three FREE GIFTS Worth $481.97

FREE Gift #1

(a $47.97 value)

Dr. Charley Martin's "Time vs. Money" DVD

This 10 minute DVD will show you how to understand and conquer the time vs. money dragon that locks you down and put a ceiling on your income and denies you the freedom to work by your rules, the way you choose.

Free Gift#2

(a $197.00 value)

A FREE subscription to my...
Affluent Practice Systems Newsletter

Accelerate your business' success and fill your brain with the juiciest, most profitable practice building secrets and strategies by getting your hands on this newsletter each and every month. Always insightful, often daring, sometimes hilarious, get you and your business juiced with the actionable ideas you'll find in my APS Newsletter.

FREE Gift #3

(a $237.00 value)

An INTERVIEW OF Dr. Martin conducted by Dan Kennedy on selling to the affluent, persuasion and conquering the sales stoppers. This is one you'll want to listen to several times over.

To learn more or to get your
3 FREE GIFTS worth $481.97, simply go to
www.CharleyMartin.com

How to Transform Any Struggling Mortgage Business into a No-Fail, Money Generating Machine...While Working Less Than Ever Before...

Michael Miget

Phenomenon™ STATISTICS

March 2006 – Started Miget Marketing Systems with no list, no customers, no marketing, no nothing. Had just 5 members.

July 2006 – Implemented lead generation ads, sales letters, website, bought ad space in trade mags, etc.

November 2006 – Held first seminar marketed to mortgage brokers and added 65 members representing $1,167,660 in revenue.

April 2007 – Repeated this process for next seminar and went to 80 members which represents almost $1.5 million in revenue per year.

 ## Opportunities for Success

I have a marketing system that I license, area by area, to mortgage brokers. Wrapped into this is on-going support/ coaching and a Mastermind component where members get my help and the help and support of other members in the program. They get periodic faxes, monthly group Mastermind calls and three Mastermind meetings per year.

Basically, I teach mortgage brokers how to use "debt-elimination" to market for mortgages. They get my knowledge of "who" and "how" to target the right prospects, which list to use, what types of marketing to use (such as direct mail, display advertising, etc.), what to present, how to present and, ultimately, I provide mortgage brokers with an opportunity to have an additional stream of revenue, separate from the mortgages they are doing, for their business. Often, this additional revenue will offset their marketing costs, making their "cost of acquisition" for the mortgages they are doing, virtually free.

Business Today

I have two businesses, a residential mortgage brokerage and a coaching/consulting business catering to mortgage brokers. These businesses are run "side-by-side" as separate entities. I develop marketing strategies, marketing campaigns, and marketing pieces for my mortgage brokerage—test and implement them there—then, roll them out to my client members in the coaching/consulting business.

Both companies are systematized. These systems are designed to leverage myself and the other resources in both businesses. So, for example, in the mortgage brokerage, most of what I do is the marketing. This is systematized so the ads are placed, direct mail sent out, responses come in, follow-up marketing materials sent out and clients developed without me having to touch anything. There are systems for all these things to happen without me having to be directly involved.

The same is true of the coaching/consulting business. I still work full-time, but running two companies, so each company is essentially part-time. This isn't possible without leverage. Also, I don't do anything I don't want to do or arguably shouldn't be doing. I hire consultants and others to work with me on stuff I hate or stuff I'm not good at.

Turning Points

1. Your business can be whatever you want it to be. This is one of the most profound ideas I've come across yet. I first heard this from Dan Kennedy. You can engineer your business to suit you instead of the other way around. You just have to decide what you want it to be, and then set things up to produce that result.
2. Take what you "do" and find the real business hidden inside of it. Most people want to think of what they do by the product they sell. This is rarely the right way to go about it.

You've got to figure out what it really is that you are selling, what the real business is. You redefine what you do, in terms of that business. Also, by doing this, it makes your business unique, since no one does this. You redefine so you are #1, the only one.

3. Use of consultants to do what you can't or should be doing. I learned this early on at the accounting firm, since this is essentially what I was to the clients I worked on. For some reason, many people are averse to paying for knowledge and information that they don't have. To me, this doesn't make sense. They seem to be okay with paying for services or having a job performed for them, but put less value on information.

4. Systems. I'm a big fan of systems. This is really a two-pronged subject. The first aspect is the planning aspect. It's extremely valuable to have a "game plan" that's proven, so in any given situation, you know how to handle it.

5. Leverage. I've talked a lot about this so far, but it's an important topic and one of my significant turning points. Most people understand the idea of hiring employees to do work for them, effectively increasing the amount of business they can do as compared to being on their own.

Money Making Strategies

People are making dump truck loads full of money doing what I do where they live. Some are even making more than I do, I have to say. I don't know if I should name names, but I've got a fellow in Chicago who immediately doubled his fees on his existing pipeline after attending just one Mastermind meeting. It was one simple mindset shift, which unlocked hundreds of thousands of dollars worth of business a year. After his first full year with me and being part of the Mastermind group, he nearly doubled his average fee per loan, while decreased the number of loans he was doing by twenty percent. He still increased his income almost fifty percent and we are talking about these percentages in relation to big numbers. He is a one-man show with very little overhead, so most of these benefits went straight to his bottom line, moving him well into the upper six-figure income range. He's happy with me.

The Phenomenon™ Applied

My understanding is that in whatever you are doing in life or trying to accomplish in life, whether it's playing a sport, learning a particular subject or running/building a business, forward progress isn't made in nice, straight, pretty lines. You have periods of time where no progress is made, a few times where you went backwards, and times where you made forward progress. In addition to this, there is a very special time where things seem to just "line-up" and everything goes right and huge, tremendous gains are made in a very short period of time. Some people would attribute this to accident or luck, but actually Dan has named it, The Phenomenon™. The trick is identifying it when it happens to you and more importantly identify what behavior or conditions triggered it to happen, so you can make it happen at will.

The Next 12 Months

The short answer is, "whatever they set their mind to!" I built a million dollar business in less than twelve months. I've had members double and triple their businesses over the course of a year. Someone could become a certified debt-elimination expert using my program in their area, gain the expert positioning that comes along with that, ability to add an additional stream of revenue to their business, increase fees on the loans they are doing now, mine the hidden fees that are currently sitting idle in their past client list, and using my strategies, be able to close deals that wouldn't be closed otherwise.

Words of Wisdom

I believe I've said it all, but I would like to go back and reinforce what I've found to be the most important thing, and that's taking action. Even if you aren't sure of what to do, or if you aren't sure what you are going to do is correct, do it anyway. Can't steer a parked car. It's much easier to correct a course that is wrong than it is when you aren't moving in a direction. In fact, you can't. Get some activity going, create some momentum, and then search out others who can help you achieve your goals. This is what I do for my members. They get what they need to get going, then we steer them down the correct path. The key is to do something, do anything.

10 Steps to Success for the "Phenomenal" Mortgage Broker

STEP 1: Figure out what business you're really in, what business it really is. The business you think you are in is rarely the business you ought to be in. You've got to get out of the product business, which in our case is the mortgage business, and get into the solution and results delivery business.

STEP 2: Decommoditize yourself by developing a really great "unique selling proposition." The mortgage business is a commodity business. Prospects can't tell the difference between mortgage brokers, thus tend to buy based on rates/fees. In reality, there is little difference between the products offered between you and your competition, so you'll need to find something unique to offer or a unique way to describe what you deliver to clients.

STEP 3: Re-invent and/or re-engineer your business to implement steps 1-2. To implement steps 1-2, it requires a re-engineering of your business. It's a paradigm shift from what you are used to and opposite from what you are doing now.

STEP 4: Find a manageable niche inside your new business. You can't service everyone and even if you could, you don't have the budget to adequately communicate to everyone. Find a manageably sized niche to focus on, something you can build a USP around and deliver on.

STEP 5: Use emotional direct response marketing to promote yourself and generate leads for your product or service. This is critical. Without leads, you have no business to close. Most brokers fail when it comes to marketing because they try to "one-step" close leads on the phone. It's all or nothing with them, and if you operate your marketing this way, it's costing you untold sums of cash—without you even knowing it!

STEP 6: Use systems to leverage your available resources. I have a system for everything in my business. From running ads, to getting mail out the door, to handling incoming leads and the marketing that goes out to them, you need systems to ensure it gets done and gets done correctly and timely. Preferably, this is automated so you don't have to do it yourself. CRM is big in this respect, as are utilizing sales letters, e-mails, faxes, letters, etc. An outsourced assistant or part-time helpers can do this for you as well.

STEP 7: Become the expert to achieve expert positioning and/or "celebrity status" within your niche. This is a natural by-product of doing emotional direct response marketing correctly. Using information in your marketing process creates a natural positioning for you with your clients. It also helps create differentiation and separation in the marketplace (decommoditize, see step 2) because almost no one does this.

STEP 8: Deliver extreme value and take the premium position within your niche to achieve premium pricing. Most people never think about any and all the ways they can deliver extreme value to a client. They are too focused on doing more business. Take the time to answer this question for yourself and it will slide you into the premium position in your marketplace, thus enabling you to charge premium prices.

STEP 9: Hire a coach and/or consultant to fill in any gaps you may have in accomplishing the above and keep you accountable and on track. The absolute biggest mistake I see people make is not getting help when they need it. This either kills the project they are working on or, at best, they get inferior results. To get the best results, you need the best input, so on things you aren't the expert at, find one and get the best.

STEP 10: Take action and implement fast! 'Nuff said.

Michael Miget, the man who has led the mortgage industry to achieve amazing marketing results with his done-for-you marketing systems and coaching programs, is the owner of Shelter Mortgage and Miget Marketing Systems. Known as the "10-Million Dollar Man" of mortgage marketing, he started a marketing system/coaching/Mastermind business for mortgage brokers in March 2006 from scratch. By November of that year, he was up to 65 members. This is no small feat, as the fees for membership are $1497 per month ($17964/yr), making this a million dollar business in just a little over a half a year. By March 2007, he was up to 80 members, making it a $1.5 million business in just a year. Michael's personal Interests include weight lifting, movies, 80s music, and architecture.

Are You Ready To Learn The Marketing Secrets That Will Have Your Mortgage Business

Making More In The Next 12 Months Than In The Last 12 Years?

Let Me Put You on the Fast Track by Sending You Absolutely FREE of Charge a 73 Minute CD Entitled

"How to Reinvent Your Mortgage Business for Increased Profits and Less Competition"

BUT HURRY…I only have 125 of these FREE CD's so ACT FAST!

Allow me to help you get a step closer to The Phenomenon™ experience by sending you this CD for FREE, **no s & h, no hidden anything!** Just me discussing my process of business reinvention, identifying customer problems you can solve and some interesting marketing techniques to position yourself as a problem solver. For me, this information and business change has meant millions of dollars in fees over the last few years, plus better hours. *Now that's something we ALL want!*

PLUS, hear me answer questions from Loan Officers *just like you* who are looking for ways to take their business to the next level, reduce frustrations and start making the kind of money they have always dreamed about.

I lay it all out on the line during this call. It's the cold hard facts about running a highly successful Mortgage Business that the rest of the guys won't or can't tell you. You don't want to miss out on this FREE CD offer. It could be the missing link you have been searching for!

"Get the mortgage business you have dreamed of without drastically increasing your marketing budget and your work hours."

Let me share my secrets with you so you too can achieve more in the next 12 months than in the past 12 years. To be one of the fortunate 125 who will get a copy of my CD simply

Go to:

www.MortgageMarketing.com/Phenomenon™

It's that easy! But hurry…once these CD's are gone…that's all folks! Don't miss out.

Stop Wasting Precious Time and Money with Unproductive Behaviors Learn How To Quickly and Easily Achieve the "Millionaire Mindset" and in 12 Months or less you too can experience The Phenomenon™

Lee Milteer

Phenomenon™ Experience: I have had two major Phenomenon™ Experiences in my career. The first one happened in the early 90s when I started working for Career Track presenting seminars to corporate employees. From this one opportunity I began to receive referrals to very large corporations for in-house training, conventions and association meetings. Then because of working with such large successful corporations I found that people were hungry for material that empowered them to reach for the dreams they had and not to settle for what others had to give them. I created a two cassette Audio Program and Video titled: "Success Self Programming," which all 120 other speakers sold at the back of the room in the hundreds of seminars that Career Track offered all over the world. Due to this one product my income jumped from $50,000 to over a quarter of million dollars in one year. Suddenly I went from a starving speaker to a well to do speaker and suddenly because of taking the risk to create new materials book publishing agents and speaking agents started to chase me to write books and to speak in very large conventions.

My second Phenomenon™ experience is still in progress and all started with a phone call from Dan Kennedy. That call resulted in the Millionaire Smarts® Coaching Program which I supply a done for you coaching program to other Niche Market Coaches, Associations, and franchises all over the world. Today we have over 16,000 people who monthly get the Millionaire Smarts® Coaching Program

Phenomenon™ STATISTICS

1986 – Traveled to over 100 cities a year presenting public and private seminars plus sale of products, and royalties income of $250,000.

2004 – Went into coaching business on the advice of Dan Kennedy which increased my income to $350,000.00 with a combination of speaking and the sale of my products, TV and Radio appearances.

2007 – Earning over a million dollars a year from the sale of OVERCOMING UNPRODUCTIVE BEHAVIORS systems, Millionaire Smarts® Coaching Program, Working with Glazer-Kennedy Peak Performers coaching, speaking, license fees, and other royalties from products.

Opportunities for Success

First, as an author and speaker I supply support to people around the world with my books and educational programs. One of my most successful programs, "Overcoming Unproductive Behaviors," has assisted people to new levels of success, productivity, and prosperity because I have helped them eliminate unproductive behaviors, habits, and beliefs that have held them back in the past.

The other support I provide is as a productivity coach, speaker, and author. One of my greatest benefits is to sell to "centers of influence" type clients who already supply information or coaching in a niche business field. My Done-for-You-Coaching program called The Millionaire Smarts® Program does the work for the other professional coaches.

The Early Years

After a number of years as a speaker and author, I began to feel the burnout of constant traveling and speaking. I was losing the passion for my work. The travel simply took most of my creative energy and within two weeks after 9/11, all my big contracts canceled. I knew I had to find a new way to create security in my world. At this time I re-released my famous Habit Busting

System that had been so successful on TV and the radio, and expanded it into two versions: One for the general public, and one version for entrepreneurs.

At the same time, Dan Kennedy approached me with an opportunity he saw within his Mastermind group. He called to tell me that he had a couple of professional niche market coaches that had a challenge, and they needed a solution. He explained to me that they needed a Professional Human Potential and Productivity coach to assist them with their existing coaching programs to reduce arbitration, increase sales, and the most important thing, to take work off of them each month.

He told me his clients found that it was easy selling the coaching programs, but it was not so easy to manage and to produce new material monthly and that these folks (niche coaches) weren't experts on the other side of success, the right thinking part of success, like I was. They were experts in the field. They could deliver great marketing. They could deliver great technical advice for their members, but they could not deliver the "get your mind working right" thinking stuff. Most important, these guys needed someone to help them lighten the load each month. So, I created a DO IT FOR THEM kind of program…the Millionaire Smarts® Coaching Program.

Business Today

Today, my website is filled with educational books, CD, and DVD programs to assist people in achieving their dreams and goals, and that has afforded me the luxury of staying home on the beach and not spending my life traveling as a speaker. I only now speak a few times a year, mainly with existing clients who are sponsors to my DONE FOR YOU coaching program, the **Millionaire Smarts® Program**, in their conventions and boot camps for business owners, entrepreneurs, and professionals. I have a small office building with four staff people but I mainly work from my home on the beach writing and preparing information for my coaching program and adding new information products to my website. I am also enjoying working in television providing materials that can assist anyone wanting more success in life.

Turning Points

My first huge significant turning point was realizing that being a speaker and author is not a real business. Wow, that was a serious wake up call. To find out I wasn't really in charge of my business but instead, the state of the economy was really hit home to me.

A second discovery was that what people REALLY want in today's world is SOMEONE ELSE TO DO THE WORK FOR THEM. Wow, this discovery inspired me to create the DONE FOR YOU COACHING Program. And the system **OVERCOMING UNPRODUCTIVE BEHAVIORS** changed my life from many hours and stress each month to massive financial security. Another turning point was realizing I had something to offer that was worth big money. I personally charge more than almost any professional in the world today per hour for my time, and people are thrilled and happy to pay me to bring solutions to their problems. That is another important breakthrough – anytime you assist anyone to get what they want, they will pay you royally for it. Another huge breakthrough for me was selling license agreements for others to use my materials, books, reports, tele-seminars, and educational materials in other countries. It was like getting free money. I had already created and sold these programs here in North American and now I could, with no work, resell them to an entirely new audience. For example my **OVERCOMING UNPRODUCTIVE BEHAVIORS system** materials are now used in many countries around the world.

Money Making Strategies

First, let me say that everyone will always get different results depending on the type of business, niche, their own experience, what they have to offer or sell, and how good they are at marketing. No one can actually put a money amount on my kind of coaching business or producing an information business. With that said, I do know people making as much as three million dollars with large coaching programs and I know people making as little as a hundred thousand or less. There are no limits except the limits of what you are willing to do to earn that income. Again, there is no ceiling to what you can earn in the information business or coaching business.

The Phenomenon™ Applied

The Phenomenon™ really happened for me when I realized I could use all of my existing experience, talents, and skills in an entirely new way. I could use all of my speaking experience, writing experience, and one-on-one coaching experience and create a service where I supplied an entire coaching program for other coaches to take work off them every month and also help the members of these groups learn to use their potential. So, I get to use my talents in a new way for a massive amount of money and an easier lifestyle where I don't have to live on the road. I can write and record from my own home and office.

The Next 12 Months

- First, get your head on straight, meaning clean up your act. Stop wishing for life to change and actually start to take action on doing what you love. Have a passion for what you really love to do and feel you can assist other and take some intelligent risks! If you have old habits, fears doubts and behaviors that hold you back, face those dragons and get them out of your life so you have the mental, physical, emotional, and spiritual life energy left to be creative and see new ways to live your life!

Words of Wisdom

Life is NOT a dress rehearsal -- it's a live show! You owe it to yourself to put on your best possible performance. And to do this, you need to lose the bad habits that are keeping you from success. Period.

Top Ten Unproductive Behaviors

1: Life-Removing Personal Habits

They include any unwanted habits that detract from enjoying life.

2: Life Removing Business Habits

These include reinventing the wheel, not being open minded and resistance to change, among others.

3: Wasting Time

As an entrepreneur, time is your only true currency. You have to get real about who and what gets your time, talents, skills, resources, and life energy.

4: Fear of Taking Risks

You must become an effective risk taker because progress in life is always going to involve risk.

5: Fear of Criticism

So many times in life we would like to try new things but we're afraid of what criticism we might receive. Listen for truth in criticism and don't take it personally.

6: Fear of Failure

The only time you really make a mistake in life is if you continue a behavior or a strategy that doesn't work.

7: Being a Perfectionist

As an entrepreneur, there is no "perfect." Striving to be perfect creates unrealistic expectations, pressures and problems.

8: Not Investing in a Lifetime of Learning

In his book *Think and Grow Rich*, Napoleon Hill says the people he studied were life time learners and always curious and open-minded about new ways to do business, seeing trends, and allowing the brains of others to assist them in outrageous wealth-making.

9: Worry and Doubt

Whether you know it or not, success in life comes from the way you think. Your emotions create your behaviors and your subconscious mind will produce what you ask it for.

10: Loss of Time Integrity

Allowing others to waste your time, using your time in unresourceful or unproductive ways at work. Not honoring yourself to be able to say NO at appropriate times.

Go to **www.milteer.com** or to **www.unproductivehabits.com** for easy solutions!

* * *

Lee Milteer is a performance and productivity Coach professional speaker, author and President of Lee Milteer, Incorporated. Her involvement with the Profit and Productivity Coaching Program has made her an invaluable asset to the Glazer-Kennedy Peak Performers team. She lives in Virginia Beach, Virginia on the Chesapeake Bay at the mouth of the Atlantic Ocean. Her personal interests include painting, photography, reading, walking on the beach, traveling, horseback riding, and working with animal rescue groups. Lee lives with her husband Clifton Williams and her Dog Angel and the Rescued Cat -Midnight.

Lee Milteer is available on a limited basis for Speaking Engagements: Call her office at: 757 363 5800 or Fax inquires to 757 363 5801 or go to www.leemilteer.com for more information.

Are You Ready To Learn How To Put An End To The Unproductive Behaviors and Bad Habits That Are Keeping You From Achieving The Phenomenon™ Waiting To Happen In Your Life?

Allow Me To Send You…NOT ONE…but
TWO FREE GIFTS Worth $207.00

FREE Gift#1
"Goal Setting for Wealth for Entrepreneurs"
This 23 page Special Report shows you how to set goals for real wealth from an entrepreneurial perspective. You'll learn…

- 12 areas of your life that you must focus on for success for balance and wealth.
- How to set goals that fit your personality.
- How to set goals that meet your inner and outer needs.
- How to create a lifestyle that makes your dreams come true.

FREE Gift#2
"The 18 Secrets That Turn Dreams Into Reality"
This report will share with you the secrets that all successful business owners and entrepreneurs use to manifest success in all aspects

of their life from career to personal. This report goes beyond main-
stream knowledge on how to set goals by giving you usable and easy
strategies that will give you an edge on your competition and make
you non-stoppable on your quest for your dreams. Discover...

- How to THINK, FEEL, AND ACT like a millionaire or whatever your dream is.

- The 5 types of life energy and how to use them. Plus have self control and manage your life energy to take intelligent risks and action using the 5 types of life energy.

- The importance of FEELING your success and having passion and vision to manifest it.

- How to know your priorities, create clear strategies, create a support system, why it is imperative to have the accountability system set up and how to be conscious of current reality for opportunities!

You Too, Can Easily Break Free From The Shackles of Unproductive Behaviors and Bad Habits (and Finally Be on Track to Fulfill Your Dreams) in 21 days (or less) Guaranteed!

Go to www.unproductivehabits.com and receive these
two FREE REPORTS that will help you break the
cycle of deeply entrenched, lifelong habits -- forever.

Best Opportunities Today in Making More and Working Less in the Highly Profitable World of Real Estate

Rob Minton

Phenomenon™ Experiences: I consulted with Dan Kennedy in October of 2004. The lessons learned in this single meeting would later turn me into a 36-year-old millionaire. Thanks to Dan, I experienced The Phenomenon™ by deciding to stop doing everything 99% of all agents do and everything I didn't like. No open houses. No showing homes. No discounting commissions. I started working only with investors.

In just twelve months, I went from struggling, doing just 84 transactions, to a whopping 270 transactions last year alone. My business income soared from $400,000 to $1.4 Million. Then in just twelve more months, I went from one brokerage to having affiliated "Income for Life" offices in 65 different cities across North America (including Canada). Generating well over $2-million in yearly revenue!

Opportunities for Success

I teach real estate agents how to niche their businesses to work with real estate investors. In fact, we clone my highly successful real estate business in their market place. I help them create their own turn-key "Income for Life" membership in their area.

Agents launching "Income for Life" have use rights for my entire business system including, lead generation, sales letters, client retention strategies and they can co-author their own version of my "Income for Life" book. Each month, I provide them with a national "Income for Life" newsletter and audio CD. They charge their "Income for Life" members fees and create new continuity income streams for their business, too.

The Early Years

I went to college for accounting. I graduated with an accounting degree and started to work for Deloitte and Touche, one of the largest public accounting firms in the world. I became a CPA and was on the partner track. A few of my clients at the accounting firm were real estate companies. I was able to see the numbers on some of their investments. This led me to start investing in real estate on the side.

I decided to get my real estate license so I could find my own investments. A few of my coworkers at the accounting firm heard about my investing. Next thing I know, I'm helping them find and buy properties using my real estate license. I really enjoyed real estate and was bored to death with accounting. So I decided to leave the accounting firm and sell real estate full time.

My business went from a net loss with no real value to a massive income with substantial value. The best part is that Dan and I were able to completely eliminate prospecting. Most agents spend hours cold calling prospects, hosting open houses, going to referral meetings and soliciting their sphere of influence for clients. We use lead generation advertisements and high-powered sales letters. I can literally drive new clients into my office through automated marketing. In fact, prospects now have to "apply" to become one of my clients. I now have hundreds of prospects applying each year to be my client.

Business Today

Today, I don't even run my business anymore. I have hired a president to run the day-to-day operation. I have a full-time marketing director who handles all of the marketing activities and five full time sales agents. I do not sell any homes. I simply manage the business from my home office working just a few hours a week because it runs on autopilot. I realize this might sound impossible for a real estate agent, but it is true. You can call my office – I promise I won't be there.

Turning Points

1. The power of selecting a niche – pick one target marketing and let all other opportunities go. (ALLOWS YOU TO CREATE A COMPETITIVE ADVANTAGE)

2. The value of a strong sales letter – The sales letter I wrote for my real estate sales business has generated well over $2,000,000 of income. (ALLOWS YOU TO AUTOMATE PROSPECTING)

3. Become the "EXPERT" – Being an expert by writing a book and gaining publicity makes a significant impact on prospects and clients. (ALLOWS YOU TO CONTROL YOUR TIME AND YOUR COMMISSION RATES)

4. Impact and power of participating in a Mastermind group – I have been in Mastermind groups with Dan Kennedy and some top business owners throughout the country for the last three years. These groups have had a tremendous impact on the way I see and go after opportunity. (ALLOWS YOU TO SEE BIGGER OPPORTUNITIES)

Achieving Success

Agents launching my system receive tested and proven marketing materials. I had to spend months testing and tweaking all of our marketing pieces. I now guide agents in running a few of my "magic" advertisements. They then send my "magic" sales letter to investors who call into their office. We prepare customized new club materials for them, which they give to their new clients. They have my entire Investor Attraction and Retention System customized and working for them in about fifty-nine days.

The Phenomenon™ Applied

When you apply Dan's strategy of massive action to your business, a point in time will come when you have more opportunity in twelve months then you did the previous twelve years. This twelve months is The Phenomenon™. The best part is that it can be planned and engineered in advance. In order to experience The Phenomenon™, a person must focus on a few key principles. You must eliminate any and all distractions, negative thinking, and naysayers.

People will tell you that you're crazy. You must also be willing to do whatever it takes. This means working like crazy to spur the actual experience. The first step is doing the exact opposite of what everyone else in your industry is doing. We decided to stop working with sellers, taking listings and helping regular buyers. Everyone, including a few of my team members thought I was crazy. They didn't think it would work. By letting these unproductive clients go, we instantly had more time to focus on attracting better clients. I studied our businesses income and found that eighty percent of our income was coming from just twenty percent of our clients. These clients were real estate investors.

We simply decided to build our niche around our top most profitable clients. Most agents build their businesses around their bottom, least profitable clients. You must utilize the 80/20 Rule to experience The Phenomenon™.

The Next 12 Months

We created a club or exclusive membership for our investing clients. An agent launching our business model could very easily have 150 to 200 members in their own club. Our investor membership has three levels. The signature level which we charge the investor $29.95 a month. The VIP level which we charge the investor $99 a month and a Platinum level which we charge the investor $199 a month. In fact, their club membership should look something like this:

- 150 total members in 12 months (this is only averaging 12.5 new members a month).
- 5 at the Platinum Level for an annual passive income of $11,940.
- 15 at the VIP Level for an annual passive income of $5,940.
- 130 at the Signature level for an annual passive income of $46,722.
- The agent launching my business model would also charge each club member a $200 enrollment fee. This would generate an additional $30,000 of income.

This means that the real estate agent would have created four new passive income streams providing $94,602.

However, the most lucrative part of the club is the commissions earned on home sales to club members. Forty percent of our members buy one home. This would lead to sixty additional home sales over the course of the year. Depending on home prices in their marketplace, this could provide commissions anywhere from $270,000 (avg. commission of $4,500) to $525,000 (avg. commission of $8,750). In addition, roughly 24% of our club members buy multiple homes. On average, this 24% buys four homes. This would lead to an additional 108 sales and bringing in anywhere from $486,000 to $945,000 in commissions.

Words of Wisdom

The turnover in the real estate sales business is rumored to be around 80%. This means that for every 100 new agents that get their real estate license, 80 leave the business. I believe this turnover occurs because the majority of real estate agents copy a failed business model. When they get started, they copy what they see all the other agents doing. This means that they are copying failure. Copying failure will not lead to success. The reason agents fail is because they try to be everything to everyone. Agents go after and try to list every type of home, from starter homes, to trade up homes, to luxury homes. They solicit condo owners, apartment owners, waterfront homes, and even listings outside of their geographic market area. In addition, they do the same thing with homebuyers, too. This does not give them any advantage over their competition. To be successful selling real estate, one must draw a line in the sand and build their business around one particular niche. This is how you engineer The Phenomenon™ in your life.

9 Steps to Success Using my Proven Real Estate Marketing System

Here are the 9 Steps you need to follow in order to experience The Phenomenon™ in your real estate sales business.

STEP 1:You must select and target a niche. You cannot be successful trying to be everything to every client. You must set yourself apart from the competition. Select a target niche and build your entire business around your niche.

STEP 2: Become an expert. Purposefully create the perception that you are the one and only expert to your selected niche. If you are perceived as the true expert, prospects will literally chase you down to be one of your clients.

STEP 3: Write a book. Write a book catered to prospects in your selected niche. Promote yourself as an author to your niche. This book will give you automatic "expert" status.

STEP 4: Create an exclusive program/club for your clients. Create a club or membership for your clients. Your club would obviously be created around your selected niche. Clubs and their exclusive membership make your clients feel special.

STEP 5: Send a monthly newsletter to lock your clients to you for life. I send my club members a twelve-page newsletter each and every month. This newsletter is funny, entertaining and educational. They actually look forward to my newsletters.

STEP 6: Use long copy sales letters to compel prospects to become your clients. I have several sales letters for my business. These sales letters deliver new clients to our door each and every week. These sales letters have completely eliminated the need to prospect for new business. My sales letters have generated millions of dollars of income.

STEP 7: Create new passive income streams in your business. If your business is entirely dependent on commissions, you're in trouble. Build additional income streams into your business to protect yourself.

STEP 8: Build your business around a future bank of sales. Each home we sell today will bring two new future additional sales in two to three years. This simply means that we have designed our business to automatically double every two years.

STEP 9: Find and participate in a Mastermind group. Mastermind groups have helped me see major opportunities for my business.

Rob Minton is broker and owner of the Paramount Wealth Group working exclusively with real estate investors. He also owns Minton Publishing, helping other real estate agents clone his real estate system, "Less Clients More Money." He was recently recognized as the fourth fastest growing real estate business in northeastern Ohio and is the author of Income for Life, Renegade Millionaire Strategies for Real Estate Agents and co-author of Dan Kennedy's Wealth Attraction for Entrepreneurs. Founder of the "Income for Life" program *which teaches investors how to buy and profit from buying nice homes in nice areas, he most recently launched "Less Clients, More Money" system in 2005, which generated $1,074,276 of revenue in 2006. Rob enjoys family time and traveling, running, especially adventure racing. He is married to his college sweetheart, Lesley. They have two daughters, Hannah, 9, and Kate, 5 and currently live in Willoughby, Ohio. The family also owns a vacation home in Myrtle Beach, South Carolina.*

Stop Struggling To Get Clients... Stop Working Yourself To Death and Get On Your Way To Making More In 12 Months Than You Have In The Last 12 Years

Let me send you a lengthy, detailed FREE report: "How I Made $90,487 Selling 20 Homes to One Client in 12 Months", which tells my whole story and...

How I get people to apply to become clients How I have over 400 clients locked to me and buying multiple properties, so I have guaranteed monthly income; How I operate never doing listing appointments, open houses, etc.; How I train my clients to work with me on my terms. And I'll send you PROOF of exactly how much money I'm making.

PLUS with this FREE Report, I'll also send an Audio CD of Dan Kennedy and I discussing my System.

So are you ready to experience The Phenomenon™ for yourself? Here are 3 easy ways to get started and get your Free Report & CD and book:

1. Call 1-888-845-9670 and enter ID 593 and leave your name and mailing address and mention you heard about this in The Phenomenon™

2. Complete the form below and fax to (440) 918-0347

3. Or simply visit **www.LessClientsMoreMoney.com**

It's that easy! Don't keep beating your head against the wall doing listing appointments, open houses... all the traditional stuff that just doesn't produce.

Dentists...Stop Working So Hard for Average Profits!

Discover How You Too Can Learn My Proven Secrets to Building a Massively Successful Dental Practice, Start Seeing a 30%, 50%, even 65% Profit Increase and Skyrocketing Referral Rates...All While Taking More Time Off and Enjoying Your Practice Like Never Before!

Ed O'Keefe

 **Phenomenon™ Experience:** My experience came when my back was against a wall. I had very little money and deep down inside was hoping someone would come along and fix my problem. Out of that frustration and desperation I threw together a teleseminar selling a product. In less than a week, I literally doubled my sales. Most importantly, I had a glimpse of what potential was sitting there the entire time; I just needed to tap into it.

My most recent Phenomenon™ experience has happened in the last twelve months. I once again doubled my business. It was the direct result of adding three more income streams into my current business and launching them SIMULTANEOUSLY.

Phenomenon™ STATISTICS

2002 – Launched Dentist Profits, Inc in late 2002. In the first four months in business, I had
generated over $200,000.

2003 – The business did approximately $800,000.

2006 – Just three years later the business did over $3.3 million.

2007 – On track to do over $6.5 Million.

Opportunities for Success

I have two overall goals. My number one goal at edokeefe.com is to inspire people of all backgrounds: business owners, sales people, athletes, parents, and any other individual seeking to achieve goals in their life. Also, I want to teach the real secrets to attracting what it is you want in you life and overcoming the invisible mindset barriers that people place in front of them by giving them the right tools, strategies, and belief systems to take themselves to heights they've never imagined before!

My number one goal at Dentist Profits, Inc is to provide the resources, tools, Masterminds, and systems for allowing dentists to increase their practice production by fifty percent, increase their personal NET profits by fifteen percent, and have an eighty percent referral-based practice!

My second goal has to do with my Masterminds and Inner Circle Coaching Clubs. I want to create an extremely positive environment where like-minded and motivated people can brainstorm, share their biggest and best successes, as well as their biggest challenges, and have other members come up with solutions.

Getting Started

My situation was a little unique, because I went into the dental profession as a marketing consultant without being a dentist. Now, the good news is that I provide a very fresh perspective and can open mental blinders that consultants who are dentists can't provide. The bad news from a point of getting started is that there is a learning curve to the insider language. However, if someone is willing to study, ask questions, and make it happen…it can be done fast.

For someone to do what I do in the industry that they already know, or a hobby they love and dive into on a daily basis, it's simply a matter of making the decision to do it and get going.

The Early Years

I was fortunate enough to go to college and get a degree, but knew that I wanted to start my own business at the age of 22. For four years, I floundered and struggled, seeking a way to make money with my own business. I tried just about everything you could imagine, motivational speaking, sales, running volleyball camps, an online Internet web store. Nothing was working. While I was still searching for the answer I went and got a job at a local restaurant and bar as a bartender. The money was decent, but I couldn't get the busy nights where the bartenders were making real money.

In truth, I was dead broke and while I knew deep down I had something that was going to work someday, I didn't know what it was or how I was going to do it. One Monday, I remember, making a measly seventy-six bucks bartending and told myself that the day my own business can make over seventy-six bucks…I'm done bartending.

Right around this same time, I came across Dan Kennedy's "No B.S. Newsletter." It was the first thing that actually made any sense from all the books, seminars, and audio series I was listening to. Now, to be fair, some of the information I studied was good and positive, but I was confused, because I was doing everything these gurus were saying. I was visualizing, I was saying affirmations, I believed in myself, and I was still dead broke.

This is where Dan's strategies were completely different. While there is still the component of having the correct mindset, without the right tools the mindset is worthless. And vice versa, without the right mindset, the right tools and strategy is worthless.

Business Today

Before **The Phenomenon**™ occurred in my life, I lived in a run down apartment that some months I couldn't afford. I borrowed money from my brothers in order to buy a round of drinks for guys at the bar. My parents lent me money. I was embarrassed about my financial situation and even though I knew I was going to be successful someday. It was still a hard pill to swallow, waking up every day with ZERO money in my bank account and expectations from people around me who cared about me, but didn't understand me.

Ten REAL Secrets To Achieving Your Goals FAST, Making BIG MONEY and LOVING EVERY MINUTE OF IT!

Step 1: Decide what you want and DECIDE to be committed. You want to make big money? Do you really want to start your own business, your own salon, your own real estate company, your second dental practice?

Step 2: Identify a profitable target market! If your goal is to make BIG money, then you have to look at a couple things before you ever get started, then the MARKET is the **#1 Key to your success.**

Step 3: Choose a business with good margins: are your margins 5X cost or 10-18 times cost? If not, then you are finding yourself in a position where you are going to limit the amount of marketing money you can spend to acquire a new customer!

Step 4: Get the knowledge you need! What knowledge or capabilities do you need? For every question you have or challenge you will face, there is a book, mentor, consultant, or seminar that will show you precisely how to handle it!

Step 5: Charge more than everyone else. Many times patients, customers, and clients will choose you, because you are charging more. They internally think, "There must be a reason why this person is charging more. He/she must be better!" Then you must deliver!

Step 6: Have others do all the grunt work for you. If you want to make forty bucks an hour or $1000/hour, then anything that falls below that range that others can do for a dollar amount that is less than that, you must work really hard at getting off your plate.

Step 7: Focus on your unique gifts, strengths, and delegate everything else. Knowing what you are brilliant at is true genius in and of itself.

Step 8: Hire the 'best' consultants and mentors. I don't know any of my multi-million dollar friends, world-class athlete friends, or anyone who has achieved greatness who hasn't hired and sought out mentors, coaches, and/ or consultants. Even when I was dead broke and didn't have the money, I borrowed it!

Step 9: Be immune to criticism. When you start achieving your goals, you will attract criticism. Look at some of our society's most successful people. Oprah builds a gorgeous school and gives young girls in Africa an opportunity – and she is criticized. **Criticism is part of the deal; so becoming immune to it is not only important**, it's vital.

Step 10: Systematize everything! The secret to creating BIG MONEY and WEALTH is to set things up, delegate, and then duplicate!

* * *

Ed O'Keefe is the author of Ten Secrets for Teen Success, The Athletes Guide to Mental Toughness, and Ultimate Volleyball Success System. Ed's personal interests include spending time with family, coaching volleyball, reading, finding new mentors, martial arts, working out, and movies. The man who has led thousands of dentists to achieve amazing marketing results with his done-for-you systems and coaching programs, first experienced The Phenomenon™ when he went from start-up to making over $6,300,000 per year all in a record breaking five years, Ed continues to recreate Phenomenon™-type achievements in his businesses time after time, but none of this was by accident. Let's see just how he did it and what we can all learn from him.

Attention Doctors....
Are You Ready To Learn The Practice Building and

Marketing Secrets That Will Have You Making More In The

Next 12 Months Than You Have In The Last 12 Years?

Get Your "FREE Special Report"

"How any Dentist can increase their NET Profits by $5,000-$25,000 a month, Experience an 80% referral based practice, while working only 3-4 days a week...EVEN during a Recession!"

(a $47.00 Value)

This 20 page eye-opening, FREE REPORT reveals:

1. The 7 Deadly Practice Killers that are sucking money out of your wallet as we speak. Yep.

   Right now! I'll show you what they are and tell you precisely how to destroy them faster than a bug would die in a FIRE.

2. 4 instant "cash flow secrets you never learned in Dental College, or from any practice management guru"…that gets new patients for you automatically, all year round!

3. An Accidentally Discovered Secret To Getting ONLY The Quality Patients YOU WANT!

4. The 3 easiest ways to practically guarantee your patients are back in your office every 6 months!

5. How to turn $300.00 bucks into over $81,736.00 VERY FAST!

6. How REAL GP's are doubling production and patient flow! How to get all the ads and postcards I wrote for them and the best way to implement each strategy!

7. Get up to 50-80% of all your new patients FREE, from referrals who all call you voluntarily!

8. The 5 almost unheard of secrets that will increase the lifetime value of each patient by 311%!

9. Secret Ways to get high quality, upper income, dream patients to seek you out – finally, end the "lowest price" types of patients wasting your time!

10. How to put your patient marketing systems on "auto-pilot" so new, high quality patients are calling you…even when you're not working! And dozens of other secrets just like these!

   Go to: www.dentistprofits.com

Make Your First Real Estate Deal in 21 Days or Less Guaranteed!

Just Think...No Sitting in Class-rooms, No Empty Promises...Only a Proven System That Is Sure to Have You Making More in 12 months or less

Sherman Ragland

 **Phenomenon™ Experiences:** In 1993, I formed a partnership to service private jets flying into Washington, DC's Reagan National Airport. On any given day, Bill Gates, Oprah Winfrey, Tony Robbins, Warren Buffet, Bill Cosby or any one of a thousand other movers and shakers would travel to this facility on their way to see the President or members of Congress. On September 11th, 2001, US Secret Service permanently shut down this $24 million per year business due to restrictions on private jet flights within a twenty-mile radius of the White House. In 2001, needing a new source of income to save my family, I turned to using "quick-cash" strategies with single-family houses. In less than 12 months, I was able to grow a second business from "nothing" to one that today generates a "significant seven-figure income" from multi-family apartments, land development and commercial real estate activities.

Phenomenon™ STATISTICS

2001 – Lost $24 million/year business.

2001-2004 – Start investing in real estate to make ends meet.

2004 – Met Bill Glazer and joined his marketing Mastermind group. Began to combine real estate investing system with business strategies recommended by Bill Glazer.

2006 – Business achieves an incredible seven-figure return!

2007 – Co-found Nightingale Institute with Diana Nightingale.

Opportunities for Success

I provide life-changing information to entrepreneurs. Specifically, I show business owners and real estate investors how to create both "quick-cash" from real estate transactions part-time, as well as how to leverage their existing business activities to acquire small-scale, highly lucrative commercial real estate investments that create passive cash-flows and lasting wealth, which can both fund the lifestyle of their dreams and be the cornerstone for generational wealth.

The challenge facing many small business owners is that 100% of their assets (and their lifestyle) is held hostage by their businesses. If something catastrophic should ever happen to their business, they're TOAST.

I learned this lesson the hard way on September 11, 2001. In 1990, my partners and I bid for and won the exclusive rights to run the general aviation facility at Reagan Washington National Airport, or "DCA" as it is better known to the professional pilots. The facility is the hangar and ramp at the airport used to service the needs of private business jets. This contract was what is known in the industry as a "total facilities management arrangement," meaning the government turned over to us a completely empty airplane hangar. We put well over $1.0 million of our own money into the building to make it ready for the private planes that flew in to Washington, DC to visit the president, members of Congress and senior executives within the federal government, such as the generals at the Pentagon, etc.

Getting Started

Truthfully, getting started in real estate can be a very terrifying experience; at least it was for me. The unknown aspects of the business are the ones that keep people on the outside looking in. TV shows like "The Apprentice" with Donald Trump don't help. The reality, however, is that most fortunes in real estate are NOT made in the glitzy downtown structures that Trump creates.

The "average size" commercial real estate deal in this country is between $2.0 million and $5.0 million and is more likely to be located "on the wrong side of town" or in a suburban location within the driving pattern of where most entrepreneurs live and where they work. This $2.0 million to $5.0 million-size deal represents about 80% of the entire commercial real estate market in this United States. These "Sherman Deals" are everywhere. Most people simply do not know how to recognize them. Guess what? Neither did I until I got started based on the need to generate $7,500 per month in less than 30 days to keep a roof over our heads. But for having my back up against the wall, I never would have started down the path that, ultimately, revealed the truth that people need to know to really be successful in real estate.

Looking at what we have done, and what I have taught others to do, I am completely convinced that anyone with a strong desire and an understanding of the principals of what we teach can create at a minimum an extra income of $5,000 to $7,500 per month from our quick cash strategies and close on at least one commercial property "Sherman Deal" within 12-months. A business owner who has an existing small business and is paying rent to someone else can do it in half the time! The key, of course, is getting started, or "going in motion" as we like to say.

Business Today

When we first started laying out our plan for entering the world of real estate investing in the spring of 2001, I remembered some of the things in my past that had been of great importance in the successful creation of our aviation business that could be applied to our real estate investing business. I remembered specifically as a college freshman listening to the words of Earl Nightingale, and using some of the same things he said that I used to get that scholarship to Wharton, and applying them seven years later in the building of the aviation business, and then again another twelve years later in the creation of our real estate investing business. One of those key concepts I learned from Earl Nightingale was the concept of the Mastermind. It worked over the previous 12 years in the creation of the "Number One" private jet operation in the country and from day one I knew it would work in our real estate investing system. At that initial real estate conference I reached out to three other investors who were in Atlanta from the Washington, DC area. We met at a restaurant at a hotel near my house when we all got back home later in April of 2001, and made a commitment to continue to help each other and meet once a month.

Today, that initial Mastermind Group has grown from four people into a 4,235-member organization and is one of the largest affiliates of National REIA in the United States. More importantly, DC-REIA has been recognized as having the "single greatest influence on the development of real estate investor education in the greater Washington, DC marketplace for investors from every walk of life." This is one of my proudest accomplishments in the past six years. I am routinely asked to speak at real estate investor groups and educational meetings across the country on the success of investors in the greater Washington, DC and Baltimore marketplace who have learned how to become investors through their affiliation with DC-REIA.

The Phenomenon™ Applied

The first time I heard Dan speak live was at a business growth seminar in October of 2003 in Arizona and what he said immediately started to resonate within me. All of a sudden, the things that I had heard from my early real estate mentors and endless hours of listening to Earl Nightingale made sense. Dan was not coming across with some "mumbo jumbo" hold hands and singing campfire songs way of increasing productivity. Nor was he talking about "incremental change;" no, this dude was talking about little changes that could have huge impacts on the business, and most importantly, he got me thinking about how to return to my commercial real estate roots. He showed me how to apply some of the things I knew about commercial real estate, but do it in a way that I could still get some of the distinct advantages of single-family house investing – in particular, SPEED!

The Next 12 Months

The challenge most people have to initially overcome is in answering the question: "How do I start?" There is no question that learning about real estate investing can be overwhelming because they do not teach you how to do it in school, and as my first mentor James Rouse said to me in 1984, you learn this business by doing it! The key is to have a system that teaches you how to do it at a level that if something goes wrong, you are not "put out of the game – permanently." While I am a big believer in the power of commercial real estate deals, I rarely start my students off with commercial deals – even small ones. Just like no medical school would let someone start off with a live human being, or a law school would let a first year law school student stand before a jury in a murder trial, we start off in real estate learning to crawl, walk, run, and then win our gold medals. This does not mean that speed is not important! Speed is critically important which is why my system emphasizes what you should be doing in your first 21-days.

Words of Wisdom

Dan Kennedy, creator of The Phenomenon™, was once asked if there was anything he would have done differently over the years in the manner in which he has lived his life and run his businesses. He said there is but one thing he would have changed early on in life, "I would have bought more real estate." Today he has changed this, he, too, is experiencing The Phenomenon™ in his life through real estate investing.

Real estate investing has been the primary source of wealth creation in America, even before it was "America." Today, many men and women have learned the power of combining a successful operating business (from "flipping burgers" to "flipping houses") with the power of using the business to buy real estate. By making an investment in The Phenomenon™ you have already demonstrated that you are searching for answers to how to create more income, in a shorter period of time. I suspect you are doing this to not only have more money, but to also have more time to enjoy. I have been blessed to be able to try my hand at many businesses, some successful, some not. Some were taken away because of the ignorance and deeds of others. This one thing I do know real estate investing has the power to change your life, and change it quickly. Probably faster than anything else I have ever experienced.

* * *

Sherman Ragland is known as "The Dean of Washington DC Real Estate Investors," for the significant impact he has had on assisting people in all walks of life to learn how to make the maximum amount of money in the shortest possible time through real estate investing. In 2001, based on success principals of Earl Nightingale, Sherman formed a four-person real estate investing Mastermind Group. The group, DC-REIA.com, has grown to over 4,200 members, one of the largest and fastest growing real estate investors groups in the US. He is the author of highly acclaimed, 7-Habits of Wealthy Real

Estate Investors, based on real life interviews of successful investors from his radio program, RealinvestorsTalkRadio.com™. He also creates "how-to" systems, based on his own journey of creating a solid seven-figure income through real estate investing in less than four years.. In 2007, he formed a partnership with Diana Nightingale to bring Earl Nightingale's "lost works" to entrepreneurs and success-minded people.

Are You Ready To Learn The Secret As to How You Can Make More In The Next 12-Months Than You Have Made In the Last 12 Years Through Real Estate Investing?

Get Your "FREE Special Report"

"The Truth About What It Really Takes To Create Maximum Wealth In Minimum Time Through Real Estate Investing, Starting in the Next 21-Days."

Plus... You will ALSO receive two incredible BONUSES:

INCREDIBLE BONUS NUMBER 1:

When you request your FREE report online, you'll also be invited in on my next FREE Tele-Seminar entitled: "The Secret to Making an Extra $7,500 to $10,000 Per Month From Successful Part- Time Real Estate Investors"

INCREDIBLE BONUS NUMBER 2:

A FREE Special Report entitled: "How We Made $575,000 In 12 Months - On Our Very First Commercial Real Estate Deal!" Hurry: Be one of the very first to take advantage and I will also send you on a CD, the actual interview with additional content that was used in preparing the Special Report.

I know how hard it is to get started as a real estate investor. Sometimes you just need a little help to get started in the right direction. I'm making it incredibly easy to take that first step in the right direction, because you really do "learn this business by doing it!" The faster you go in motion, the faster the rewards come, the faster you become truly financially free.

Simply go to: www.MoreWealthin21DaysFreeGift.com

Or call me at 1-800-748-0487.

Discover How ANY Loan Officer Can Easily Bring Home 6 Figures, Working Fewer Hours and Finally Start Enjoying Life Again!

Brian Sacks

Phenomenon™ Experiences: By industry standards I was one of the top producing mortgage bankers earning over $200,000.00 per year consistently. But I was extremely tired and burnt out. I found that it was a job that required my attention 24 hours a day, 7 days a week which left me with no time to spend with my family.

I first experienced The Phenomenon™ by plugging Glazer-Kennedy style marketing into my mortgage business and then using it to produce my first info-marketing product for the mortgage industry. This brought me into millionaire status, I later sold that business for over 7 figures. I have experienced The Phenomenon™ time and time again when I created three additional info-businesses that continue to bring in over six figures each month and when I founded the National Association of Responsible Loan Officers.

Phenomenon™ STATISTICS

Late 2002- launched www.loanofficersuccess.com, his first info-business to mortgage professionals, generated $85,000 in just a few months.

2003- increased sales to $575,000 and doubled that in 2004.

2005- sold the original mortgage info business for over 7 figures

2002-2005- created 4-5 additional businesses that each now produced high six figures each and every year We interviewed Brian Sacks, the man who has led thousands of loan officers to work less, make more and achieve their dream lifestyle with his proven systems and strategies. Brian has experienced The Phenomenon™ several times throughout his career but this was not by accident.

Getting Started

It is almost too easy to get into our industry but thankfully that is all starting to change. For many years, in most states anyone could become a loan officer with very little training and no qualifications or tests to take. In my case that was actually good news since I barely graduated high school. But in reality it is scary to think that a potentially unqualified and untrained person who may have been homeless yesterday is now working on a persons largest lifetime purchase.

The Early Years

I started out as a Realtor in 1984. I was actually doing well as a Realtor when the manager of my office decided to open a mortgage company and took me with her. Remember, back in the 1980's rates were in the teens but we were still doing a lot of business...just more creatively. It makes me laugh looking back when I hear loan officers complaining when rates go from 6-7%. That company didn't stay in business very long and so I went to work for a bank. Ironically, after being there about 4 years, this bank was taken over by the US Government during the famous Savings and Loan Crisis. I then went to work for a mortgage banking company and rose from being a loan officer to a branch manager to a regional manager in charge of offices in various states. After 10 years this company was sold to a bigger company and I went to work managing a local mortgage brokerage shop. After a short while I found the owners were totally unethical and were actually condoning fraud. I immediately quit and decided since I was really not "employable" I should just open my own shop.

Business Today

My life today is totally different. I am always at my children's school and sporting events. I no longer carry a pager and always leave my cell phone in the car where it belongs. We take at least 2 major vacations each year and most are out of the county. Best of all I have consistent and predictable streams of income each and every month.

Turning Points

The first is when I discovered Dan Kennedy and Bill Glazer and the marketing strategies they teach. When I applied them to my business everything improved…quickly. Some of the other discoveries and breakthroughs were learning that you really can design your ideal life and make your current business conform to it. Finally, you need to guard your time and make sure that you get all "You need to also realize that you are a marketer first and foremost **so you need to take the time to work ON your business instead of IN it."**

Money Making Strategies

I have put together a special page where you can find out more about all of the various resources my members and I use to benefit from these ideas. They are available at **www.loanofficerformula.com** .. Now if I were you I would ask "Ok, what's the catch?" Good question so let me answer it by giving you sort of a bonus marketing lesson. People want information and the more good information you can give, the more credibility you will have with them. It is exactly the same process that car dealers use when they offer you a test drive. Same with food companies who offer you free samples. They know that if they truly do have a great product then you will trust what they are saying. They have proved it to you. So to take advantage of your free no-strings-attached gifts go to **www.profitandwealth.com/free**

The Phenomenon™ Applied

There are certain triggers that will allow anyone achieve more in the next 12 months than they have in the past 12 years. All of us have dreams and desires that we have kept hidden or feel are unrealistic related to health, business and/or true wealth. Most people wander around aimlessly until they ultimately just give up and stop even trying to accomplish these goals when in reality, once they learned The Phenomenon™ Triggers they could actually reach those goals … quickly.

In my case I was doing fine as a loan officer earning about $200,000 - $250,000 pretty consistently each year. I was however working like a dog and was on the verge of total and complete burn out. It was just then that I learned my son who is dyslexic would need to go to a school that cost $28,000 per year and my mother would need to be in an assisted living facility that cost $48,000 per year. That was enough to jolt me into quick action. It dawned on me that while everyone around me, my wife included, was talking about how to drastically reduce expenses, move to a smaller home, cut back on vacations, never go out to dinner etc…Maybe the answer was to significantly increase my income and do it quickly. As a result I created a training company for loan officers, based on the successful strategies I had been using. It quickly grew to a multi million dollar company that provided newsletters, seminars, coaching programs, and done for you services. I recently sold that company for over 7 figures and have launched a half dozen other companies two of which have hit the million dollar mark in revenues in their first 12 months.

10 Steps to Mortgage Marketing Success

STEP 1: Know Where You Are Going – Have Written Goals

If I told you that I will give you ONE MILLION DOLLARS in cash if you can get to Kalamazoo by noon tomorrow, what is the very first thing you would do? When I have asked this question in seminars around the country most loan officers tell me that they would fly, drive, take a train etc. Problem is, most have no idea where they are going. They want to take action but have no idea what the outcome should be. You can't have general goals to succeed.

STEP 2: Make Sure You Are On –Track Your Progress

I am usually pretty good with directions but still manage to get lost sometimes when I am traveling. In success key #1 I told you about the importance of having a written goal and a plan to accomplish it. Now let's talk about the second step in this 2 step process. While it is critical to have your goal and plan you must also make sure that you are on course and have not taken a wrong exit or highway that will ultimately take you away from your goal. Heaven knows we are all easily distracted especially when business is good. So what you want to do is in the first week of every month review your production from last month.

STEP 3: Be Careful Who You Listen To …Get A Mentor

The one thing that is an absolute certainty in our industry is that it is full of companies trying to sell us new fangled ways of generating business. What's even worse are all of the "gurus" who have either never originated a loan or actually originated loans so many years ago that their models and ideas are outdated and worthless. We all know how quickly things change in this business. In fact that is one of the things that makes this business so exciting for me personally.

STEP 4: Don't Commit Mortgage Marketing Incest

If you are like most other originators, or any seller of services for that matter, I bet you have committed this cardinal sin of marketing…. I know I did when I first started. It is only natural to look around, see what everyone else is doing, and then do the exact same thing. The result is that we all look and sound alike. However, the bigger issue is that this causes prospects to only use price as the only distinguishing factor.

STEP 5: YOU Must Control the Buyer and The Deal

This is just simply the rule of the Mortgage Origination jungle. This one thought has the potential to totally change your business and your focus. While everyone else is out there begging for business from realtors, builders etc. you will be safe and comfortable generating high commissions.

STEP 6: Position Yourself So Buyers Are Chasing You

Please don't hate me for saying this but most of us run around like hungry dogs looking for a meal. True, some have raised begging for business to a slightly more respectable format but all in all it is still begging. When you are forced to beg for business you have lost total control of your income and quality of life. You are forced to bow to the needs of the persons who feeds you. I did this for most of my career until I wised up and learned some specific techniques to have buyers chasing me.

STEP 7: Create Million Dollar Loan Application Appointments With Yourself

One of things we are all guilty of is not making enough time to market our services. We seem to be too busy or maybe too distracted is a better word. So let's take a minute here while I ask you a question…" If you had a million dollar loan application tomorrow at 10:30 am, the buyers are not shopping you, and are already sold on using your services. All you have to do is show up. WHAT WOULD KEEP YOU FROM GOING?" Well if you are like most of the originators around the country, then your response will probably be the same, NOTHING!

STEP 8: Use Emotional Direct Response Marketing That Is Trackable and Accountable

I am constantly amazed at the e-mails I get from companies trying to sell me (and you) the newest way to get business. You know what I mean right? The company calling to sell you the side of the shopping cart you can put your name on. Or the screen in the movie theater. Or the radio, TV or newspaper ad. What's interesting is that they all say pretty much the same thing that goes like this. "You need to do _____ so that when someone is looking for a mortgage they will come to you. You need what is called top of mind consciousness". This is called "Brand Advertising" and it can work. But you need to have a six or seven figure advertising budget like Countrywide or Bank of America. If you are just a small business or just a lone originator there is simply no way to compete with your current marketing budget. The solution is what is known as Emotional Direct Response Marketing and I personally learned many of these concepts from Dan Kennedy and Bill Glazer.

STEP 9: Don't Be Too Accessible

One of the big lies I learned very early on in this industry was that I needed to be accessible all the time. It was called giving good service and was the lever I used with Realtors, Builders, and prospects to earn their business. We are in such a competitive business that the fear is you will lose the deal by simply not returning the call fast enough. In reality being too accessible can actually hurt you.

STEP 10: Pick A Niche, Become The Expert. Let Everyone Know About It… Be a Specialist, NOT a Generalist.

This one statement has not only made me famous in the mortgage industry , but has produced millions of dollars for me in commissions and closed deals over the past 10 years. I have already told you many secrets to success you can implement immediately but this is the biggest. If you are frustrated by the hours you are working, tired of the rate shoppers, tired of being viewed as a "head of lettuce" then pay attention. In a nutshell what you want is a group of buyers who have a specific need or issue and see you as the solution. Then you ONLY market to those that have that problem.

BOTTOM LINE: Pick your niche, become the expert and let everyone know about it so you can close LESS loans make more on each one so you can have the time and freedom to enjoy your life.

* * *

*Brian Sacks is the CEO of **www.loanofficerformula.com**. He has been an industry expert for over 24 years, closing over 6000 loans totaling 1 BILLION Dollars. Brian has trained thousands of originators and company owners in North America, sharing his "FORMULA" for success that will allow you to close LESS loans, Make More Money and Have a Life REGARDLESS OF MARKET CONDITIONS. You can read his FREE 32 page special report entitled The Death of Mortgage Origination As We Know It & The Little Know Things You Must Do Now To Survive and Thrive by visiting **www.loanofficerformula.com***

*This report has been downloaded by over 9200 originators and company owners, may investing $97.00 to learn these little known, tested secrets! So grab your FREE COPY NOW as a gift while it's still up at **www.loanofficerformula.com***

Are You Ready To Learn The Business Strategies and Marketing Secrets That Will Have Your Mortgage Business Making More In The Next 12 Months Than In The Last 12 Years?

Then Let Me Give You A **Complete Tool Box of Resources** *that Will Allow You to Start | Implementing the Tips and Strategies You've Just Read About.*

Just Go To www.loanofficerformula.com

and get immediate access

Stop Working So Hard. Start Learning
How to Close LESS LOANS, Make More
Money and Finally Have Time To Enjoy Life!

Not a loan officer but still wanting to learn the secrets of success. Grab 2 FREE GIFTS- NO STRINGS ATTACHED! These are 2 Classics that every successful person MUST HAVE in their library. Grab yours at www.profitandwealth.com/free

How Anyone Can Build a Wildly Successful Online Business Regardless If You Know Anything About Computers or the Internet

Yanik Silver

Phenomenon™ Experiences: In 1987, at the age of fourteen I stated working for my father's medical equipment company. I struggled to find my place in the business world until I came across direct response marketing. Marketers like Dan Kennedy and Earl Nightingale changed everything for me. In just a few short years, I went from average to a millionaire, all on the Internet, all before the age of 31. Then just twelve months later, I achieved The Phenomenon™ again with business topping $3 million. Now, I coach and teach others to achieve The Phenomenon™ in their own lives. However, if you ask me what's the most important aspect of The Phenomenon™ experience, I would most certainly say the incredible lifestyle I now enjoy, something I proudly call "The Internet Lifestyle."

Phenomenon™ STATISTICS

1998 – Started first information marketing business selling to a small niche of 10,000 prospects produced $150,000/ year while still working full-time.

2000 – Launched www.InstantSalesLetters.com, which did $1800 in the first month, continues to produces six figures per year.

2004 – Becomes a millionaire at age 31.

2005 – Business tops $3M+ and that's with zero employees except wife, Missy.

2007 – Attendees pay up to $10,000/per person to hear Yanik's Internet moneymaking secrets.

Opportunities for Success

In a nutshell, I show people how to find, develop and then sell products and services online. Not only that, I have created a system that basically does it all for them IF they follow my lead and plug in my proven system.

It can be very difficult for the beginner starting off in the online world. You read and hear so many things that it's hard to know where to focus and what to do first. You can spend thousands on your site and services but still not see the kind of results you desire. I have to tell you, when you have the right guide – you can experience tremendous success in a very short amount of time and not break the bank in the process.

The Early Years

I started at 14 working for my father's medical equipment supply company. And at the young age of 17, I was a serious student of marketing and spent hours a day studying experts such as Dan Kennedy and Earl Nightingale. I put their direct marketing techniques into action with dad's business and they pulled very, very well. I then started doing the same kind of work, on the side, for a Dermatologist. Success again. I figured I could show other doctors how to do the same and my first info-product was in the works. Within a year I was doing about $10,000 a month. Then it hit me…what would happen if I created more products and sold them online, but products like e-books, with no product cost and no delivery charge.

Problem was, I was a computer dunce. My friends were rolling on the floor laughing when I told them I was going to put up a website. And they had every right to be amused since I had absolutely no website design skills, zero HTML or coding knowledge. In fact, not much computer "know-how" whatsoever (still don't).

Basically, my first product idea came to me in the middle of the night. At 3:00 a.m., I woke up with an idea and quickly got up and registered the domain **www.instantsalesletters.com**. I remember the first e-mail telling me I had $29. The first month I did $1800, then $3600, $7200 in the third and $9400 by the fourth month. It was in that fourth month that people started asking me what I had won and I started teaching others about Internet marketing. The rest you could say is history, but I still continue to profit off that first site and now have well over 12 other sites as well.

Business Today

Personally, the Internet Lifestyle means being able to do pretty much whatever you want, almost anytime you want, and letting the Internet pay for it!

Truth is, never before have we lived in such a time filled with immense opportunity to do your own thing…quickly and easily. The Internet has truly been a revolution for anyone that wants to either "Moonlight Online" or go at it full-time and make a solid six or seven-figure income.

Turning Points

1. Realizing the same skills I had offline would easily transfer online as soon as I saw a profit model I could follow.

2. Setting up the value system of "*I get rich by enriching others 10x – 100x what they pay me in return.*" I always try to think of how to add exponential value for any product or service I sell.

3. Good direct response marketing can leverage all your activities and set you free from one-on-one sales.

4. You get to set the rules for how you want your business and your life to run. Stop relying on the conventional wisdom on a 9-to-5 existence waiting for happiness at the end of 40 years!

5. Never being paid for time put into a job. Get paid over and over again for work done once. Leverage everything you do for multiple paydays.

6. Realizing the difference between succeeding and failing is simply using "idle time" to prepare for the opportunities coming my way.

The Next Step

I have many choices for those interested in starting an online business. I have what I call my "Fast Track" to online success, which allows you to choose the path that interests you. I have tons of e-books and products, which are all very affordable and packed full of the precise tools, tips, and secrets that I use and many of my students have used to create massive wealth. On rare occasions, I speak about Internet marketing. You will find my schedule as well as all my resources and tools at **YanikSilver.com.** Oh, and be sure to check out my personal blog **www.InternetLifestyle.com** for my thoughts on fun, freedom and financial freedom!

The Phenomenon™Applied

Creating The Phenomenon™ in my life, or what I like to call, my Internet Lifestyle allows me to do and enjoy things that are far beyond just the money benefits. Here are a couple things off the top of my head what the Internet Lifestyle means to me:

- Having money come in on autopilot while I sleep.
- Doing the work once and getting paid over and over again.
- Never answering to a boss.
- Having your accountant perplexed and surprised when you see him each year at what you do and how much it brings in.
- Working with who I want, when I want.
- Not living for the weekends.

The Next 12 Months

Don't be put off by starting. When I first started, my friends were rolling on the floor laughing when I told them I was going to build a profitable website. And they had every right to be amused, since I had absolutely no website design skills, zero HTML, or coding knowledge; in fact, not much computer "know-how" whatsoever (still don't). But, that didn't stop me from going ahead with my simple two-page website, and the flood of orders hasn't stopped.

You must have goals looking forward and at present. I use the Franklin Covey planner system and I highly recommend it. You can create long-term goals, intermediate goals, all the way down to your daily task lists.

Ask yourself: Where are you going? Be specific. Write it down. Don't be afraid to write it down. Now, how are you going to get there? Get those intermediate goals set up first. If you get the little building blocks going it's a lot easier to get to where you want to go.

8 Steps to Success With Yanik's
Sure Fire Marketing Systems

Here's a quick glance at what you need to do to build a highly successful Internet business:

STEP 1: Come up with products that solve a problem. Everyone has a problem. Find one and meet that need by offering them a solution…your product.

STEP 2: Create compelling copy that sells. Unless your site gets the job done, you can't go ahead with the activities that will bring you in the big money. Spend as much time as you have to getting your site to consistently convert visitors to buyers.

STEP 3: Make your site a direct response order-taking machine. Most people mistakenly try to put a lot of free stuff and content on their site. It's not necessary. Almost all my sites consist of one long sales letter (and yes, people do read it all and buy!)

STEP 4: Keep going back to your buyers. It gets easier and easier as you go along because the real big money is in continually coming out with products your existing buyers want. Don't start from scratch every time trying to sell your product.

STEP 5: Share the wealth. One of my biggest secrets is using an army of commissioned salespeople on the Net. They are my affiliates. I only pay these affiliates when they make a sale so you can potentially have hundreds – even thousands of affiliates driving traffic to your site.

STEP 6: Deliver more than you promise. I always try to deliver just a little more than I promise with some kind of free unexpected bonus to my customers.

STEP 7: Joint venture. Once you know your numbers (like conversion percentages, visitor value, etc) then you can approach people with a joint venture proposition. You're looking for people with big databases that you can tap into. Your goal is to get an endorsement from them. Don't be afraid of giving them the lion's share of the profits either; you'll get it back with all the business they will bring you.

STEP 8: Start an affiliate program ASAP. After you've done several joint venture deals on an individual basis, you'll want to open up your program to the world. Let other people sell your products for you and you pay them only when they sell.

* * *

Yanik Silver is the owner of **SurefireMarketing.com.** *Starting from his one-bedroom apartment and with just a few hundred dollars invested, Yanik and his wife Missy have personally sold over $14,000,000 online and counting. He's sold everything from e-books on fitness, and houseplants to over $20,000 Mastermind programs. He drives more traffic to his homemade, barebones sites than huge multi-national conglomerates. He's been featured on the cover "Millionaire Blue Prints" magazine, inside Business 2.0, TIME.com, USA Today, Financial Times, Delta Sky Magazine and Denver Business Journal among others. Yanik and Missy live in Potomac, Maryland with their two children.*

FREE 1 Month Charter Membership – Underground™ Secret Society

"Now Each and Every Month, You'll Get My Most-Guarded Underground Internet Marketing Secrets, Strategies, Research, Ideas, Private Contacts, Cases Studies, Tools, & Resources…That I Am Unable To Reveal Anywhere Else"

- Jumbo-sized, jam-packed newsletter. The information is so unique and private I am only ever opening the doors to 925 subscribers ever (and it might not even get that big). Each month the Secret Society newsletter turns out to be 3x or 4x the size of most other people's newsletter.

- Full length Audio Interview on CD with a new unknown Underground success story. Not the same usual suspects and not people making their money pushing "how to make money online" info. I have loads of insiders on my "hit list" who owe me a favor or two and I plan on collecting by interrogating them and picking their best information out of their head. You'll get a complete unedited and "raw" audio CD of our candid interview. Plus, a complete word-for-word transcript with your audio.

- CD-rom with Web Site Reviews & Critiques. I'm going to give you full-blown, confidential access to different copy critiques I've given real customers on real sites. You'll see their websites as they were submitted to me and then you'll see the exact, point-by-point advice I send back to them! PLUS - You'll even have the opportunity to submit your site in for review and critique as a Secret Society Member.

- Bonus call-in days. I normally charge $750/hour for private phone consultation. Throughout the year, I'll set aside significant blocks of time only for Secret Society members. You'll get a private call-in number to get a hold of me.

- LIVE, closed-door mastermind meetings for Secret Society members & much more!

You have to see everything in store for you and the best way I know how is to let you try it all. That's why I've set up a special 1-month charter membership to the "Underground Secret Society" reserved ONLY for you here:

www.UndergroundSecretSociety.com

That means the burden to deliver is on me. You've got a full month to profit and enjoy all the benefits of your charter Underground Secret Society membership. Once you get your Secret Society printed material and audios, go through it all, check out everything, listen to everything and then see what you think. If I don't deliver – I don't deserve your money. You're the sole judge, jury and if need be, executioner.

Get all the details and sign up for your FREE trial before the next issue is mailed because we NEVER sell or make backissues available.

www.UndergroundSecretSociety.com

The Truth about Making $400,000.00, $800,000.00 or even $1,000,000.00 per Year in the Mortgage Industry!

Scott Tucker

Phenomenon™ Experiences: I was fired by my broker on December 18, 2001. I wanted to stay in the mortgage business, but didn't know how to get my own deals. I had to learn emotional direct response marketing on my own, lead only by those willing to teach me, such as Dan Kennedy. Within three months, I had learned what I needed and had implemented it. I spent $5,000 on my first mailing, and crossed my fingers. Since I needed money coming in, I mailed all 5,000 pieces at once, which was nuts. The very next day the phone started ringing off the hook with mortgage borrowers beating my doors down to work exclusively with me. Back then, I had no assistant, and I worked out of my then one-bedroom loft condo. But no matter, 'cuz after two months, I had closed all those loans from that 5,000 piece mailing, and I had made fee income of $75,000!

In the spring of 2004, I told my story to Dan Kennedy in a coaching meeting. At that time, I was making $500,000 a year in fees, working just under 40 hours a week. Dan told me that all that was impressive and that I ought to offer it to others in the mortgage business. So I launched my program for other loan officers/bankers/brokers, and within 18 months, I had 165 Members paying me $1497 a month for my system, coaching, and advice! That's $3-million a year!

Phenomenon™ STATISTICS

1998-1999 – went from $25K a year to $152K a year, in just 12 months by implementing Kennedy marketing techniques.

2001-2002 – went from $152K a year to $442K a
year, again in just 12 months simply by continuing to develop & perfect his marketing system.

2005 – moved up to $731K a year by launch-
ing program to other loan offices

Present – $3-million a year– and having the time of his life!

Opportunities for Success

I provide my marketing system for reverse mortgages to loan officers and
brokers all over the US and Canada. They are able to darn-near instantly
increase their incomes, from $4K to $6K, in one example, to $80K per
month. There are several examples and testimonials of results similar to this
one.

Getting Started

Most people in the mortgage business got into it when times were easy. A
"refiboom" is when most folks get in. During a refiboom, borrowers are
plentiful, and you can get some deals closed in spite of yourself. You'll have
enough deals to close, that even in spite of price buyers, carved-up fees, and a
lack of supporting marketing materials, you can keep the lights on.

When rates rise, or an appreciation bubble bursts, is when most folks in
the mortgage business get into real trouble. Some only then realize that they
need a marketing system that makes them immune to "rate" and "price." I
get folks joining my program in good times, and in bad. What's so exciting is
that my system works in any market conditions…even in otherwise "tough"
markets.

With my marketing system, they can totally change their lives within
as little as 30 days, but certainly within 12 months. The marketing delivers to
them reverse mortgage borrowers that are ready, willing, and able to pay any
price, accept any rate, and to work only with my members.

The Early Years

I finished my degree anyway, and moved to Chicago to work for a
friend in his mortgage brokerage. He was making really big money, and the

mortgage business seemed just right for me. It's a challenging profession that offers great compensation, flexible hours and casual dress.

But although many in the mortgage business make the big bucks, most starve. And, even those high-earners usually only earn the big bucks in a "refiboom."

When I was later fired by my friend, in 2001, just a week before Christmas, I realized it was time to get real smart about a marketing system – how to get borrowers to chase me, to be able to sell a loan no matter what "rates" and "fees" were – no matter what I saw fit to charge.

That's where Dan Kennedy came into my life. He's the one guy I've learned the most from. Not only in marketing systems, but in achieving The Phenomenon™.

Business Today

I went into the office today for five minutes this morning, but I don't need to be there the rest of the day, because my assistant, Tiffany, has it all covered. This is a pretty typical day for me.

I'll just work from home, on my couch, using my laptop, for the remainder of the day that I choose to put towards work. And all my evenings are free, just as I got them to be in my mortgage brokerage using my system.

Turning Points

I'd have to say that the single biggest "tactic" that made all this possible is the discovery/ revelation that it's possible to put a system in place that causes people to chase you and throw their money at you. I don't mind working, but it's just awful to be in sales or in business, or both, and have to wonder where your next meal is coming from. With a marketing system, the business chases you. And price is no object in your prospects eyes either, which I know sounds ridiculous to those who haven't experienced this first-hand.

But onto the "strategy" part…another big breakthrough is the realization that I can, at will, snap my fingers, do a few things, and double, triple, quadruple my income. Nowadays, I do so at will. That really sounds nuts to people, but that's what happens!

After I figured out how to do it the first time, it's like lather, rinse, repeat! I don't even have hair, but I get that! And I'm able to do this whenever I want. It's just a matter of do I feel like working hard for few weeks to pull it off. That's The Phenomenon™!

Money Making Strategies

Some people do better than others, but those who do the best job of just applying my system as instructed are blowin' through the roof. It's up to the individual really. Some just want to make $200K a year, which to me sounds kinda silly, cuz so much more is possible, but everyone has different goals.

Getting Started

Step 1: Get your marketing ordered/placed/deployed. This can be a mailing done for you by one of my vendors, or a free-standing insert (FSI) in the paper. My system has all these components in template form and ready to go with a simple, "edit, replace" function in Microsoft Word.

Step 2: "Your phone" gets answered by the service I set you up with. And, your website collects online applications for you while you sleep. You sit back and have the leads pop out the other side to your e-mail inbox or to your fax machine.

Step 3: You work up a "deal" for the borrower(s). You call them back and tell them how you can help them.

Step 4: The borrowers drive to your office to meet with you, sign-off on your forms, all that.

Step 5: The borrowers drive to your office a second time for the closing.

Step 6: The title company FedEx's you a big fat commission check. A lot more than most loan officers and mortgage brokers get paid.

The Next Step

The next step is to go to **www.MortgageMarketingGenius.com**. There you'll be able to learn a whole lot more about my marketing, my system, and my program. You'll see and hear from members of my program. They'll tell you, in their own words, what this is all about, and how it can work for you.

The Phenomenon™ Applied

It is a bit hard to put into words but by using The Phenomenon™, darn near anything is possible. It is possible, to tie together a number of things, all at once.

"Normal" people do one thing at a time. They work all alone instead of with others of like minds. Phenomenon™ Practitioners bring several things together all at once. In fact, we often work with one another, here and there, formally and informally, to achieve more and more all the time.

The Mastermind Group can be as small as two of us. Or it could be 24. It can be any size, just so long as all involved are committed to the goal.

The Next 12 Months

I'm saying that a loan officer or mortgage broker can, using my strategies, all of which capitalize on The Phenomenon™, achieve more in income, have more time off with their family life and all that in the next 12 months than they've been able to achieve in the past 12 years, even now! That's the 12-timesing I'm talking about. This Phenomenon™ of 12-timesing things is The Phenomenon™ itself! I've done it, I've seen countless others do it countless times! Shouldn't you be next?

10 Steps to Success with My Tucker Reverse Mortgage Marketing System®

It might be immodest to say, but let me just get it out in the open: a whole lotta people in business, in general, and in the mortgage business, in particular, marvel at my success. Disappointingly, most only marvel. Only a select few ask me "how to" questions, which are immensely more valuable questions, and more fun to respond to than just a plain old compliment.

STEP 1: Whatever business you're in, get yourself a mentor, coach, somebody who has *proven* success in that business. And by that, I do *not* mean someone who is in business for 30 years and just finally had his first good year. I mean somebody successful without a lifetime of B.S.

STEP 2: Get yourself a Mastermind Group of likeminded butt-kickers. Not the whiners from the water cooler. Not the dorks from your state brokers' association continuing education class. At least not the majority of the folks you find there.

STEP 3: Find yourself effective marketing materials that have been tested and proven to do what you want to do. I do not mean buying postcards from the next marketing company that e-mails you. I mean finding effective marketing, not just "marketing."

STEP 4: Get yourself exclusive marketing materials. It doesn't do much good to scream "me too!" in your area. You need to be the only guy sending out the marketing you send out.

STEP 5: Keeping in-line with STEP 4 above, you cannot be screaming "lowest rate."

STEP 6: You cannot be screaming "lowest fees."

STEP 7: What you can say is that you get things done that no one else can. Sound dishonest? I don't think it is, so long as you promise me you'll use your noggin'. I find that fully 50% of the borrowers that apply to my members have been turned-down by an average of three other brokers!

STEP 8: Your marketing can't say "mortgage" all over it, because people have an "oh, yuck" reaction, and they tune it out immediately. Get this right, and you, like my members, will have 50% of the people applying with you to be folks that have no prior inquiries to their credit reports!

STEP 9: Move quickly. Money is made fast, not slow. Get your prospective borrowers in and out lickity-split. They should be closing no more than three to four weeks after first contact with you. Yes, this is possible.

STEP 10: Take chips off the table for your own savings, investments, IRAs, wealth accounts, and charities. Doing this will yield amazing results in your life that you cannot fully appreciate until you do it and see for yourself.

These are exactly the ten steps to success that I've followed, and they've worked like a dream for me. All ten are necessary for any of them to work to great effect. If you'd like more information on my program and reverse mortgage marketing system for loan officers and mortgage brokers, please go to **www.MortgageMarketingGenius.com** right now.

* * *

Scott Tucker is the owner of Tucker Marketing Systems, a company that provides reverse mortgage marketing and coaching to loan officers, mortgage brokers, and mortgage bankers. Known for having been a very successful mortgage broker, creating $731K a year in fees, working part-time, with just one part-time assistant, and never needing to leave the office to do it, he now licenses his system to other mortgage brokers, throughout the US and Canada. Scott is the author of Marketing for Mortgage Brokers and Reverse Mortgages…from Z to A, co-author of Dan Kennedy's Ultimate Sales Letter, Ultimate Marketing Plan, Wealth Attraction for Entrepreneurs, No B.S. Direct Marketing Walking with the Wise Entrepreneur, and Ruthless Management of People & Profits. His personal interests include dogs, muscle cars, Harleys, boxing, and hockey.

"Are YOU Ready To STOP dealing with Realtors, start doing FEWER loans... and still end-up making TWICE-AS-MUCH CA$H-PER-MONTH?"

I know it may sound too good to be true, but I did it & scores of my Members have done the same! I think it's time you learn these secrets, put 'em to work in your mortgage business, & start enjoying the good life, instead of spinning your wheels in frustration!

When you go right now to **www.MortgageMarketingGenius.com**, and give me your contact info, I'm gonna give you a 100% FREE Special Report that reveals all the details to you! You'll see & hear from my Members, in their own words, exactly how my System works, and how it's made them a ton of money! All while working LESS!

You're going to learn just what makes my System better than ALL the rest...and don't worry...you won't just be listening to me go on & on...you will actually hear from my Members who are using my System to predictably, reliably, and repeatedly get $10,000.00, $20,000.00, even $25,000.00 checks! On every deal!"

That's right, my Members will tell you about their very own successes, and they'll "spill the beans" on me & my System, and how it works! And the best part...It's 100% FREE!

Don't let past experiences with other so called "gurus" stop you from taking advantage of this incredible 100% FREE offer! And keep in mind, it doesn't matter:

- Where you live!
- Whether or not you have any reverse mortgage experience at all!
- What your split is!
- What your state cap is!
- Whether or not you have to have an attorney present at your closings!

> *What does matter is that I'm going to show you EXACTLY how you can experience The Phenomenon™ for yourself, and get on your way to making more in the next 12 months than in the last 12 years...*

Go to www.MortgageMarketingGenius.com & sign-up for this totally FREE Special Report right NOW!

The Truth about Making Big Money with Real Estate Investing... Just Imagine, in 12 Short Months You Could Be Making More by Working Less Than Ever Before

Tim Winders

Phenomenon™ Experiences: In the summer of 2001, I was at the end of my rope. My consulting business had slowed almost to a complete stop and financially I was in a huge hole. I hit my knees and prayed for something that I could be passionate and excited about every morning when I woke up and got out of bed. Three days later I was sitting in a real estate seminar. One year later I had purchased 36 houses. Thirty-five months later I had purchased 110 properties, total value of 12.7 million and the business has continued to grow.

Phenomenon™ STATISTICS

2002 – Twelve months after introducing Dan Kennedy's Renegade techniques, Tim purchased 36 homes generating income of $227,602.

2003 – Purchased 74 properties for a total value of $12.7 million in real estate holdings, boosted income to $754,417

2005 – Started a support business for real estate investors to help them generate leads from motivated sellers, which skyrocketed his income to $1,723,665.

Opportunities for Success

I work with real estate investors that desire to have a strong, successful, fast growing real estate business. I show people how to add $100,000 in income and $1,000,000 in net worth in 12 months. I can work with people that are just getting started in the real estate business and I can show the seasoned investor how to increase their profits and put their business on autopilot. I am a systems engineer from Georgia Tech by training, so I can help investors set up a real estate business that runs like a well oiled machine.

Getting Started

There is a perception that it takes money and good credit to start buying and selling houses. When I started my credit was shot and I had no money. In some ways I think that was a good thing. I was forced to be creative. Anyone starting in real estate can be successful and create money and wealth for themselves and their family if they get started and stay focused.

The Early Years

I had a degree in engineering and had worked in the corporate environment for nine years. I worked in a little cubicle even though I held the elite title of manager. I spent almost two hours every day fighting the rush hour traffic. I am still not sure why they call it rush hour. In Atlanta, you just sit still for almost an hour. I had attempted a few business ventures with moderate success, but those businesses started slowing down and I soon found myself with over $100,000 in credit card debt and a negative $6000 per month cash flow. I was tired and frustrated and, quite honestly, did not know where to turn. I wasn't at the end of my rope. It had been some time since I had even seen my rope!

Business Today

I spend about one hour per week working on and in my real estate business. It is running on its own because I have put a team of people in place and automated systems that can keep the business going and growing. I still talk to sellers that want to sell their homes, because I enjoy doing that part of the business. Our business is holding steady at 85-90 properties. We sell a property every few months and we purchase on average about one property every month.

I am passionate about coaching and teaching others to succeed in their business. Most of my business time is spent working with students that are in the process of creating wealth and freedom for themselves. I work with a limited number of students at any given time and I provide customized coaching and mentoring for their specific business. That's what really sets me apart from the others out there…customization.

The Phenomenon™ Applied

I think there are two critical pieces to experiencing The Phenomenon™. The first piece is the mindset that one must have to achieve more in a short period of time. It's unfortunate that most of what we program our minds with will produce the exact opposite of the results we really desire. I have really focused on what I read, who I listen to, and the people I associate with.

The second piece that contributes to The Phenomenon™ is massive, focused action. Notice I did not just say action - being busy all the time. The action must be focused toward the results you are seeking. That does not mean you will have an exact picture of what your business will look like. Your picture will become more crystallized while you are moving. It is nearly impossible to fine-tune a business plan while you are standing still. As my real estate business was growing, my main goal was to buy three houses each and every month.

The Next 12 Months

For anyone reading this, they can absolutely change their life in the next 12 months. You are only limited by what your mind can conceive.

The process starts with a decision. It cannot be a timid decision. It must be a powerful decision. In the summer of 2001 I was at a crossroads. I was a broken man that was on the verge of financial destitution. I made a powerful life changing decision to attack life and be passionate about whatever God put in front of me. That catalyst caused the phenomenal explosion and I absolutely believe that the same thing can happen to anyone.

Words of Wisdom

Over the last few years I have worked closely with, or coached over 2400 real estate investors. From 1990 until 2001 I worked with over 3000 small business owners all over the world. In far away places like the Philippines, India, Romania, and even Alabama. I kept noticing trends related to success. Some people just seemed to have it all together; while some seemed to never even get started on their path to success.

I started realizing there were some basic truths to success. The main thing that I have observed from studying thousands of successful people is this: success is a process, not an event.

7 Steps To Success

STEP 1: You MUST focus on marketing. There is a reason I devote a large part of my time to teaching marketing. Every vehicle needs some form of fuel to make it go.

STEP 2: Don't be lazy. We live in an instant society where hard work has almost disappeared. Most people need to just do more. Get busy. Hustle. I doubt that Sam Walton worked "nine to five" days. Check your schedule and see how much actual productive work you are doing in your business.

STEP 3: Get educated. Most people reading this spent at least 12 years getting a basic education. Some even went on to get additional degrees to learn a trade or skill. Always be in the learning mode. Read, attend seminars, and have an open mind.

STEP 4: You MUST commit. Many people lack commitment to anything, so we should not be surprised if they lack commitment to their business. If you are not sold on your business and yourself, what makes you think someone is going to pay you $8,000, AND let you take over the mortgage?

STEP 5: Don't be cheap. There is a difference between properly managing money and just totally shortchanging your business. Anything worthwhile requires investment of time and money. Guess what? That is a big fat lie. You must invest money in your business.

STEP 6: Don't expect business results from a hobby. If someone has a hobby, they know that it will cost them money and will never yield any profit. Don't let real estate be a hobby. It will be very expensive and frustrating.

STEP 7: Stop being a lone ranger. You can only reach a certain level of success all by yourself. It may sound very impressive to proclaim that you are a self made man, but I must admit I have never met nor seen anyone that is actually self-made. You need to surround yourself with a team of people that can help you achieve big things.

* * *

Tim Winders is involved in real estate investment, real estate coaching and training, and creating support businesses for real estate investors. He is the author of The Freedom Equation, 40 Days to $5000, How to Get Your Private Money Pipeline Flowing 40 Days to Becoming a Deal Making Machine, How to Analyze Deals in 90 Seconds...Or Less, 40 Days to Becoming a Better Husband, How to Put the Spark and Sizzle Back in Your Marriage with Lori Winders, 40 Days to Becoming a More Treasured Wife, and How to Put Spice and Sparks in Your Marriage with Lori Winders and is also known for training packages, "Hold That House" and "Fast Track Wealth System." Tim and his wife live along with their son and daughter in Lake Oconee, Georgia. His personal interests include starting new businesses, running, boating, spending time with family, traveling and relaxing. They also spend time doing ministry working with married couples, as well as, writing and speaking on this topic.

Are You Ready To Learn The Real Estate Investing Secrets That Will Have You Making More In The Next 12 Months Than You Have In The Last 12 Years?

Get My FREE 7 Step eCourse "How to Create a House Buying Machine That Will Put $5000, $25,000, $50,000 or More in Your Bank Account Each and Every Month" AND Test Drive My Real Estate Inner Circle for ONLY $1

This Free 7 Step eCourse reveals my step by step guide that shows you exactly how to easily buy massive amounts of houses AND create a house buying machine. Here's a quick peek:

- How to get motivated Sellers to call you
- What type of marketing gets the best results
- How to pre-qualify every seller that contacts you... without even talking to them
- Magic phrases to use on the phone
- The art of buying houses without leaving the comfort of your home
- Questions to ask the home seller...and questions to never ask

- And much, much, more…

PLUS, because I know you are hungry to experience The Phenomenon™ for yourself I want to offer you one more very generous opportunity.

When you go to **www.realestatephenom.com** I'm going to give you this FREE Course and I'm going to also throw in… A 21 day trial to my 'Real Estate Inner Circle' for ONLY $1 (a $79.90 value)

With this my Inner Circle Membership you will have instant access to:

- Over 100 articles - new articles added monthly
- Real world real estate transactions dissected and reviewed before your eyes
- Monthly audios - Freedom Fighter Interviews – I personally interview successful investors and business people so you can "listen in" on the latest tips and techniques that are being used by the elite investors in the country.
- Members Only discussion forums monitored by super successful investors
- Inner Circle audio and video training valued at $694
- New and Improved Members Only Website
- Special Inner Circle Coaching Call In Days

* After trying my Real Estate Inner Circle for 21 days and seeing how these incredible tools and powerful information transforms your business, you can continue your membership for only $39.95. More information and details on the website.
Incredible opportunities like this only come around every so often and especially opportunities that can completely re-invent your business and send you into that Phenomenon™ Experience we have all told you about.

Go to www.realestatephenom.com and take advantage of this $1 Special Offer before my accountant catches wind of my insane generosity and puts a stop to it.

How to Use Auto-Responder and Strong Copy to Grow Your Business at a Staggering Pace

Mark Stokes

Phenomenon™ STATISTICS

2008 – We have sold in excess of £500k ($1,000,000)

In just 6 months trading with an on target forecast of £1,000,000 ($2,000,000) for the next 12 months.

Opportunities for Success

After 15 years of corporate bullshit and directors of the same company telling me what to do against my own beliefs in business and also never being considered for directorship, I decided to promote myself to director by starting my own company called Charnwood Home Improvements back in August 2007.

After 3 months of setting up the company and putting in all the systems to take the company forward, I realized that without marketing skills and being able to acquire customer enquiries the business would fail within 12 months. So I subscribed to Chris Cardell inner circle in England and went to the entrepreneur's summit in London April 2008, that's where I met the great Dan Kennedy and Bill Glazer.

I joined their GKIC members circle, bought all their marketing material at the summit, went home and taught myself how to write copy. I worked day and night to learn about writing a sales letter. I also bought an auto responder to implement into the business, had a new website designed showing all of our products and testimonials from our existing customers, we also created a sign up box onto the home page that feeds through to a sales funnel in our auto-responder and now we have at least 15 different marketing sources to create a customer enquiry. This was the action that started off our Phenomenon™.

Getting Started

12 months ago I was working for a big corporate company in England selling home improvements. I was a regional sales manager. I'd been doing that for probably 15 years, up until 12 months ago. My brother was running a hot tub business in the UK. I always wanted to run my own business but never took that plunge.

I just felt that it was time to break away from the corporate world and set up our own business. I went into partnership with James, my brother.

We set the company up over a three month period. We rented a little showroom. We bought all the stock on our credit cards. There were no phones to start with–we had to use our mobile phones. After three months, we realized that the business was going to fail unless we found customer enquiries.

We had to take massive action because we were going to fail.

I didn't even know what an auto responder was 12 months ago, nor did I understand what copy was all about. Auto-response, pay-per-click landing pages were the first things we had to learn quickly. I hopefully will inspire anybody who wants to start a new business after this, because I can tell you now the things we've implemented certainly work.

The thing we put in place was to buy an auto-responder. We scanned the Internet and we got various help on it. I think it's probably the most powerful tool that we actually got at the time. The effort that goes into putting the information in the auto-responder is where all the hard work is.

But we basically copied what Bill Glazer and his marketing information gave us. We literally copied it and changed it into our product. I think what Bill and Dan say is, "Get into the mind of your prospect."

And when you're writing copy, if you can get into the mind of the prospect, those sales letters that you write really do work if you concentrate. That is the key to it. We created several e-mails and sales letters, then put them into our auto-responder, transforming things for us. Warming up the prospect by sending free advice and information then contacting them either by phone or door-knock doubled our conversion rates over night.

Business Today

In April 2008, it looked like my new business would fail. But since I attended the entrepreneur's summit in London that month and began using Kennedy style marketing, my business has grown to 10 staff on payroll, along with 23 sub-contractors. Yes, the speed over the past 12 months has been staggering, but isn't that what the Phenomenon™ is all about?

All the wonderful tools GKIC has to offer, along with massive action and implementation, were the triggers to our Phenomenon™. And we plan to continue in 2009, with a forecast for three million in revenue by December of 2009.

How to Leapfrog Your Way To Success in Real Estate and Business By Leveraging the Power of Association and the Power of the Mastermind

Marlene Green

Phenomenon™ STATISTICS

1998 – Discovered Real Estate Investor Association and was introduced to Section 1031 of the tax code

2008 – $4.2M in positive cash flowing rental properties added to portfolio

2009 – President/CEO of Millionaire Blueprints Media, home of the award-winning Millionaire Blueprints Magazine

Opportunities for Success

I connect the dots for business owners and investors by giving them a reality check, by providing resources and new insights, and by sourcing 'how to' blueprints and information they can use to help them get ahead. For several years I ran real estate and business mastermind groups, did private business consulting, and provided direct access to wealthy investors and self-made millionaires willing to share their secrets to success with those eager to learn.

It's critical for investors, entrepreneurs and business professionals to always live by the Principle of Gaining a Slight Edge and be on a lifelong educational search for insider information and knowledge from those who have successfully done what you aspire to do.

I move in many circles and am a natural talent at connecting people with others who can help them. I also connect the dots for folks when it comes to sharing strategies they can apply to their business and pointing out opportunities they should pursue.

I pity any person in business who feels they are too cool for school and can't afford to take time out to invest in their education and personal development. Huge and costly mistake!

Having crossed paths with hundreds of investors and business owners, I see consistent evidence that if you invest in your education, take immediate action on what you learn, and associate with the right smart people by attending events and being part of a mastermind or peer advisory group, you are bound to experience The Phenomenon™.

The Early Years

I grew up in Jamaica where a premium is placed on higher education and lifelong continuing education. I came to the United States with that instilled in me and lived up to the stereotype of the Jamaican with 4 jobs who works really hard to take advantage of all opportunities that came my way.

One of the major goals for a Jamaican coming to the United States is to save enough to buy your own home as soon as possible and then work on buying other residential properties for rental. I held down 3 jobs in college that allowed me to travel around the world and graduate without any debt. After college I worked as a consultant for many years and earned enough to buy my own home and several residential properties.

I learned how to buy real estate by devouring books on real estate. I had no mentors, no real estate groups, no courses or bootcamps. I just had books and the sheer will and determination to work and save enough to put down 20% for each acquisition. At one point all my properties were owned free and clear because I didn't want to have any debt.

I acquired a lot of residential properties on this slow program where I learned by trial and error and attended the School of Hard Knocks in dealing with tenants and contractors. I only focused on acquiring properties to rent for positive cash flow and appreciation.

Over many years I wondered how I could go about buying multi-million dollar properties…those large apartment buildings and commercial buildings. I had no one around to ask how to do this and I had no clue where to look or how to start. All I knew was that it would take a long time to work and save 20% to put down on million dollar properties! Ah, the high cost of ignorance...

Turning Point

The turning point came for me when I learned about and attended my first creative real estate conference and saw hundreds of people from all backgrounds gathered for 4 days to just live and breathe all aspects of real estate. I had died and gone to heaven! Finally, I found experienced people who loved investing in real estate to build wealth and were willing to share their knowledge. I also met some folks there who told me about the local Real Estate Investors Association (REIA) that held meetings 15 minutes from my home.

I actively participated in the REIA and immediately took advantage of every resource available to learn about creative real estate buying strategies, financing, tax strategies, entity structuring, asset protection, and property management. I also learned about Section 1031 of the tax code that allows you to leverage your equity in smaller properties into larger properties. Finally, I got the answer on how to buy those large apartment buildings and commercial buildings. Ah, the value of education and knowledge...

I then traded up into larger properties and took it on myself to go wherever I needed to go to learn as much as I could from the real estate gurus and wealthy real estate investors who were willing to teach and share their knowledge and experiences with a newbie. Remember, I knew the cost of ignorance in the early years when all I had were books to read – no mentors, no role models, no courses, no bootcamps. Consider the time lost and opportunity cost: if I had access to those mentors, role models, courses and bootcamps in the early days (as you do now), how much more could I have accomplished?

My mindset and my thought process changed once I internalized how wealthy investors think and operate. I felt privileged to learn from the best people out there who were doing for years what I aspired to do. I must add that I learned from the grizzled veterans who have been investing for decades and have tons of war stories to share about investing during different economic cycles.

Their wisdom and years of experience are priceless. I suggest you make a point to seek out the folks in your area of interest who have been around a long time. Beyond investment and business tactics and strategies, there is much wisdom and insight that you can gain from their war stories and recounting of history and the evolution of things.

As I got caught up in buying more and more real estate, I kept hearing about the importance of consistently marketing to bring in deals. It was at a Ron Legrand event that I finally got to hear from this Dan Kennedy guy that so many of the real estate gurus referred to as the guy that they go to for marketing advice. Dan did his Renegade Millionaire presentation and offered The Most Incredible Free Gift Ever. It was then that I got onto Planet Dan and went beyond the world of real estate.

On Planet Dan, I was mainly drawn to the Renegade Millionaire Strategies and Wealth Mindset as this was an extension of what I was experiencing in real estate investing. I was then introduced to information marketing and learned that we are all really in the marketing business and the asset-building business.

There are 3 Phenomenon™ Mindset Triggers that happened for me:

1. Real Estate is not my only Asset. I can also go out and build my own Herd (member or customer list and relationships) via information publishing.

2. Positive Cash Flow from Rental Income is not the only Continuity Income.

3. It is okay to Leapfrog to larger development projects, from smaller residential units. They just involve BIGGER numbers. Why should I take baby steps on small deals when I could do the same thinking with bigger numbers?

Because I benefited so much from networking and masterminding with others of like mind at events around the country and around the world, I wanted to help other "lonely entrepreneurs" save time and money and become energized by facilitating local face to face meetings. I took on running a real estate mastermind group and later a local chapter of GKIC.

Though technology allows us to connect to anyone around the world in an instant, there is something to be said for having face to face in the flesh contact with other people. It is critical to not remain isolated behind a computer screen. Get out and connect with people face to face and at local and national events. Don't ever discount the value of face to face human interaction.

The Rocky Road

My real estate journey certainly has not been without major setbacks, disasters and bumps in the road! I have been through costly litigation with a business partner, lost $1.77M on a development project where I personally guaranteed the loan, had costly mis-hires because I was totally clueless about hiring and managing people, had money go down the drain because I didn't put metrics and timelines in place to measure progress, and lost a great deal of money and time dealing with vampires (aka Lawyers, Bankers, Contractors, Tenants).

I share some of these experiences and harsh lessons learned in business in my *Screwed In Business*™ book and audio series. I think we must have honest conversations, ask tough probing questions, and get a reality check on what business is *really* like. *It is not all smooth sailing, though many make it seem like it is.*

Very few successful business owners and investors share the bad stuff that has happened to them for the benefit of instruction to others. I am changing that by asking everyone I know about the bad stuff that happened to them, how they dealt with it and what they learned. I learned very early that you must go deep and ask probing questions to get at the heart of any issue. That's how you learn about the REAL STUFF that will save you time, money and energy. I have learned so much from hearing the horror stories and bad stuff that my mentors and other entrepreneurs have experienced that I make an effort to heed their warnings in my own business.

But sometimes I screw up, like not heeding several real estate gurus' warnings about not personally guaranteeing loans from institutional lenders and then getting myself in a bind when the project fails and they come looking to me personally for their money. From first hand experience, I can tell you that I won't make that mistake again!

Keep on Truckin!

Despite the rocky road along the way, I have triumphed. This is only because I did the following things and I suggest you do the same:

1. Maintained a *positive attitude* despite all the bad stuff I have had to deal with and never got discouraged.

2. Remained *persistent* and *never* gave up despite several setbacks.

3. Continued to *observe closely and learn* from the best marketers and entrepreneurs around.

4. Remained *immune to criticism* of any kind because I know where I have come from in the early days and I am very clear about where I am going on my journey.

5. Consistently *invested in my education and personal development to prepare* for future opportunities that would come my way.

6. Continued to *look for opportunities* to pursue by finding hidden assets and structuring win-win deals both in real estate and business.

The Phenomenon™ Applied:

With Millionaire Blueprints™ there are many instances of The Phenomenon™ applied that you can dial into for your own business:

1. **Our Extreme Marketplace Advantage & Positioning** is that we ONLY provide *Business Blueprints from Self-Made Millionaires.*

2. **Our Profound Reason for Existence in the Marketplace** is that we 'Provide Detailed Examples & Step by Step Instructions from Self-Made Millionaires' with an extensive listing of time-saving tools & resources that our audience finds extremely valuable enough to become a permanent part of their reference library.

3. **Our Hidden Assets** are in our relationship with a diversity of millionaires, our distribution channels, and our content for other **WHOs** (Millionaire Blueprints Teen & Junior Magazines).

4. **Look at what others are doing in your Industry & Don't do it.** Most other magazine publishers do not offer <u>measurable value </u>to their clients or <u>leverage various types of media</u> strategically to attract, entertain and build an <u>ongoing relationship</u> with their Audience. We do these things.

5. **Our Business?** Not just another Magazine that sells Advertising…we really are <u>not</u> in the Publishing Business.

6. **The Power of Belonging, Celebrity and Status:** We leverage our brand name, content, connections and offerings to gain revenue from **Multiple Sources, _not just 1 Revenue Source:_** *Advertising.* (Remember that the worst number in business is ONE!)

7. **It's all about our <u>Relationship</u> with our Audience.** We have hundreds of *"Love Letters to Millionaire Blueprints"* from readers that are testimonials to the value and impact of the information and resources we provide. We pay close attention to our audience member experience by providing 'how to, step by step instructions" in many forms that they can act on.

Words of Wisdom

My words of wisdom for you fall into the four categories.

Surround yourself with great people:

- Find mentors and experts who are doing exactly what you want to do and model them. Why reinvent the wheel?
- Commit to learning from the best people out there and make the investment to travel and pay your way to learn and get access to people of influence.
- Join a local mastermind group or peer advisory group and feed your brain with good stuff every day.
- Be very careful who you Associate with and let into your Inner Circle.
- Business is all about relationships. You must nurture your relationships with peers, prospects and clients.

Make marketing your #1 job and priority:

- Know that your primary job is that of being a marketer and taking care of your members, clients and tenants so that they will take care of you.
- Watch How Your Time is Spent Everyday. It's the one thing that you can never get back!

Never stop paying attention to the bottom-line:

- Watch your numbers – always! Never delegate this.
- Focus on getting private money investors and lenders. Avoid banks.
- Ruthlessly Focus on **Profitability First & Net Cash Flow Always**, (*not Gross*). Cash Flow is Queen and Cash Is King.
- Always aim to be profitable. Many people do business or real estate deals for ego's sake and do not focus on making a profit. Focus on profits first, always.
- Know how to legally keep as much of your money as you can by educating yourself about tax minimization strategies and entity structuring.
- No matter what business you are in make it a point to acquire income properties to build long term wealth. Real estate is all about equity and cash flow, and people will always need to live and work somewhere in any economy!

Don't be afraid to fake it until you make it:

- Exude Confidence even if you are shaking in your boots! Remember, EVERYBODY had a first time doing something and had to start somewhere. Just get started. Experience and Failure are the best teachers so if you do get knocked down just get back up and keep going!
- Be Solutions-focused, not Problems-focused. Don't complain or whine as no one cares about your problems, drama or trauma. Be resourceful and only focus on finding solutions.

***

Marlene Green, Entrepreneur, Investor and Creator of the **Screwed In Business**™ *(www.ScrewedInBusiness.com) series is the Chapter Director of Glazer-Kennedy Insider's Circle's Manhattan and Northern New Jersey Chapters (www.GKICNewYork.com) and President/CEO of Millionaire Blueprints Media LLC (www.MillionaireBlueprints.com) which publishes the award-winning Millionaire Blueprints Magazine. Marlene is a master networker and connector who enjoys providing 'fresh eyes' and connecting the dots for her members and clients. She is a passionate crusader for the "Lonely Entrepreneur" and encourages you to join a mastermind group where ideas and strategies in marketing, business and life management are discussed freely for everyone's benefit. Marlene is a co-author of the* "Secrets of Peak Performers" *book with Dan Kennedy, Bill Glazer and Lee Milteer and is the author of* "Screwed In Business: 101 Reality Checks and Harsh Lessons Learned in Business that Cost You a Ton of Money, Wastes Your Time and Drains Your Energy". *With the contributions of Members of the Millionaire Blueprints' Founders Circle, the Millionaire Blueprints' Society of Millionaires, the Implementation Team and the Strategic Partners at Millionaire Blueprints Media, Marlene is committed to continue delivering the Blueprints,* "Detailed Examples and Step by Step Instructions from Self-Made Millionaires", *that Millionaire Blueprints Magazine is known for to every corner of the world.*

ARE YOU READY TO LEARN FROM THE STORIES, THE SUCCESSES, THE FAILURES, AND THE TRIUMPHS OF SELF-MADE MILLIONAIRES THAT WILL HELP YOU MAKE THE RIGHT MOVES TO BECOME THE NEXT Phenomenon™

Remember that after many years of trial and error and trying to figure things out on my own, my life quickly changed once I had access to millionaires, successful entrepreneurs and wealthy investors who were willing to show me the ropes and tell me what to watch out for and how to go about getting things done.

I want you to have the same opportunities to learn the good, the bad and the ugly directly from self-made millionaires so that you too can get a jump start on becoming the Next Phenomenon™!

Simply go to www.MillionaireBlueprints.com/Phenomenon™ to get your 3 Free Gifts from me because you can relate to my story:

Marlene's Free Gift #1:

Get your FREE Audio e-book where I discuss excerpts from my book "How We Got Screwed in Business: 101 Harsh Lessons Learned to Make Sure YOU Don't Get Screwed in Business Like We Did"

Marlene's Free Gift #2:

Get 1 FREE Digital Download of one of the most coveted back issues of Millionaire Blueprints Magazine. You get to experience an entire digital edition of Millionaire Blueprints Magazine.

Marlene's Free Gift #3:

You will also receive a special teleseminar invitation to an upcoming Millionaire Blueprints' Fireside Chat where we interview a member of the Millionaire Blueprints' Society of Millionaires. The Society is made up of all the self-made millionaires who have provided their blueprints to the Millionaire Blueprints' audience.

Marlene's Special Bonus Free Gift Offer (only while supplies last):

If you can spare $4.95 to cover the shipping, I will snail mail you another coveted back issue so that you can feel in your hands and experience an entire print edition of Millionaire Blueprints Magazine. This offer stands based on what we have left in our limited inventory of magazines published prior to 2009 so act now before we run out if you want to get one of the coveted back issues of Millionaire Blueprints Magazine sent to you.

The fastest way for you to get all this is to simply go to

www.MillionaireBlueprints.com/Phenomenon™

The Story of ILTC (International Language & Training Consultants), France

Carol Bausor

Phenomenon™ STATISTICS

2003 – Purchased company from partner
2007 – Attended "Super Conference" in Chicago
2008 – Sales up 16% and profits up 23%

Episode 1:

It's late on Friday before Christmas, 2006: no one else is in the office except me ….. I really should be going home, but I just wanted to have a look again at the document I'd just received from Dan Kennedy. I'd read all his books, liked them so much I visited the web-site; and now they kept sending me invitations to events. This one is for the Super Conference in April 2007– and it sounds just what I need. Since I bought out my business partner a couple of years ago, things had been dire … there were so many debts that I had been obliged to put the company into Chapter 11, and not a day went by without me wondering how I could have been so dumb as to buy a dying company. Would I make myself and my family bankrupt? My husband regularly reminded me that he had told me not to - and here I was, working 14 hour days, paying myself last (if at all) of the 16 staff members, and tossing and turning at night……. And wondering whether to jump in the Seine (my Head office is in Paris), or in the Rhone river (in Lyon, where I live). So what did I have to lose by gong to a Conference? I checked it out – sure, we couldn't afford it but: Inscription fee in four easy payments, the dollar was low compared to the euro, and I could always find a cheap flight. I signed up, sent the fax, and went home. Gulp.

Episode 2:

I arrive in Chicago, am amazed to see so many people! Dan kicked off the Chicago Super Conference, all bandaged up after his horse-racing accident, by saying that he imagined that some people were maybe staying at a Motel 6 rather than the Hyatt (guess where I was staying?!!! He was talking to ME!!!), and that was OK if it was their choice, but not if it was by obligation. Yes, he really was talking to ME! "If you listen to what I say" he goes, "next time you will be able to stay at the same hotel as the venue." And that is exactly what happened ...... in September 2007 in Baltimore, and always, since then ....

Episode 3:

I travelled back to France in April 2007 on a high. And I'm still way up there! In spite of my great enthusiasm, when you are managing a company that:

- Has a staff of 16, all of them overworked
- A load of debts
- Is in Chapter 11
- Has severe cash flow problems

It is by no means easy to implement all the brilliant things I was learning. But I read diligently and little by little things got better.

So let's talk about the past 12 months:

April 2007 taught me a new attitude: a can-do killer mindset which means I CAN'T LOSE! The past 12 months have intensified that. I'm so positive that my staff find me exhausting. But my clients (more and more of them on our list) love it.

We started Direct Marketing – a new one in France! In November 2007 we invented an event "British Beaujolais Night". You know, I'm sure, that the annual evening when the new Beaujolais wine is sold for the first time, is party time. And Lyon, second town in France, is considered to be the capital of food and drink. So we invented a party for something that doesn't exist: there is no such thing as British Beaujolais! But it was a great excuse for creating rapport with our customers .... And for consolidating team spirit. It was so successful that we did it again in November 2008: this time we had

200 guests, 4 new accounts, an article in the local newspaper, and a lot of good feeling.

In May 2008, inspired by Dr. Nielson, (we asked his permission to copy this one!), we sent out an invitation for a seminar to learn English with the story line about one of our trainers who overcame his fear of clowns when he had a clown for a student. And the clown was afraid of looking stupid when he spoke English. So we helped him overcome that. We had 50 enrolments on that seminar this year ......

We have hired Vince ZIRPOLI to tidy up our management style. We have read Paul HARTUNIAN on press releases (enclosed is the Press Release we sent out in September). We read every book of Dan's, refer to Mega Marketing religiously, and study the monthly newsletters. Over and over.

We sent out a mail to our customers for Christmas to introduce a new product, we celebrate their birthdays, we are constantly in touch. We refine our mailing list EVERY week. We have a Head of Marketing!

In fact, we even have our own Newsletter now.

So what are the results of all this?

1. First of all, and this has a value greater than $: people love working in the company, and our clients give us great feedback about the atmosphere in the place when they come in for their lessons.

2. We don't have a staff of 16 anymore: we have **32 employees.** Our Paris office, where I had laid off 8 people, has in the process of being built up again, and I have recruited a great Manager

3. We have a new product – not about learning a foreign language – but about changing your mind set so you can learn AND communicate efficiently in ANY language. We have no competition for this product.

4. Sales have increased by 16% BUT profits went from 3% to <u>**23%**</u>**!!!!!!!** We have a new office in Paris, and have extended our office space in Lyon. We have opened an office in Algiers.

5. I come to work every day with a smile on my face. Direct Marketing, Kennedy style, is fun.

If you want to know how to get into the right mind-set to learn a foreign language, or to succeed your objectives in **desperate** circumstances!:

Go to www.iltc.fr

carol.bausor@iltc-lyon.fr

The TrySports Story:
How you can quickly and successfully grow your own retail business!

Jim Kirwan

Phenomenon™ STATISTICS

2004 – Opened first store in Mt. Pleasant, SC

2007 – Opened 2nd store. Sales of $1.6 million, a herd (members) of 11,000 and 1500 referrals

2008 – Opened 3rd and 4th stores. Sales of $3.1 million, a herd of 20,000 and 2600 referrals.

Preface

Jim Kirwan and TrySports was the winner of the Phenomenon™ competition held in Orlando, Florida in January 2009. One of the prizes was this chapter in this book!

TrySports' Business

Let me tell you a little bit about TrySports. We would be classified as a specialty running and triathlon store. But to me we are much more than that. Yes, we are there to sell high quality products but our real mission is to create a world class specialty retail business providing added value services. But above all, and I mean above all, we are there to inspire our customers, to get fit, stay healthy and to enjoy the aerobic sports of walking, running, swimming, cycling, triathlon and fitness in general. Our motto is the words "Believe. Achieve."

Getting Started

We opened our first store in 2004 in Mount Pleasant, which is a beautiful town in South Carolina. If you've never been, I highly recommend that you go there. I met Bill actually first along the way, subsequently Dan and with their help and guidance we changed a lot of things. And I guess the changes have led to what TrySports is today.

When I started TrySports, I didn't want to be an average retail store. I didn't want to be a good retail store. I wanted to be the best. So we've set our stall out to be a world-class specialty store. And we identified four key ingredients as follows:

- Extraordinary Customer Service
- Excellent Staff
- Massive Marketing
- Best Locations

First is that we have to provide extraordinary customer service with the emphasis on the word *extraordinary*. Second, if we want to provide great service we have to have great staff. It doesn't work if you don't have great staff. Third we need to have massive marketing and forth we need to operate in the best locations that are available for us.

Phenomenon™ Triggers

I have identified 5 Phenomenon™ Triggers which together have profoundly influenced the growth and development of TrySports as follows:

- Decisions & Mindset
- Getting Things Done
- Extreme Competitive Advantage
- Systems & Processes
- Economic Advantage

Decisions & Mindset: Probably the most important decision I made in the early part of 2006 was that I needed to work on my business, not in it. And I'm now working 100 percent on the business.

Goal setting and objectives are very important in TrySports and we use the acronym SMART. For those of you who don't know what that means it is specific, measurable, agreed, realistic and timed and they're the ingredients of successful goal setting. They work for athletes. They work for businesses.

Of course, you have to manage performance so the ongoing management of performance is also critical in our business.

Getting Things Done: In TrySports, massive marketing is a catchphrase we are all familiar with and I am going to use it to illustrate getting things done. To us it means having many balls in the air at the same time. Some of them drop but most of them don't. It becomes very difficult for our competitors to compete with us when we have so many things going on at the same time.

However, we are very clear in our focus and in our priorities with respect to marketing. Our first priority is to look after our current customers who are members of the TrySports Rewards Club [probably our most important marketing strategy]. Our second priority is to get our members to refer their friends and family and that's a very clear, focused priority for us. After that and only after that we look for new customers.

Extreme Competitive Advantage: I believe we have created extreme competitive advantage in a number of ways and I want to use our shoe fitting process as an example of this, which we call *Five Steps to the Perfect Fit*. I have to tell you that it is the most comprehensive shoe fitting process in the country, and as I don't have time or space to elaborate here, I'll ask you to accept my word for that. This comprehensive process allows us to create an environment and an atmosphere in each of our stores, which is unique, dramatic and dynamic. We also have a mobile fit truck which allows us to take our F*ive Steps* process out into the community. We take it to events. We take it to races. We take it to strategic partners. We use it for chartable purposes and we are able to get great publicity from that.

Systems & Processes: This is another crucial factor in our success and the TrySports Rewards Club and 5 Steps to the Perfect Fit would be just two examples of systems and processes. We are, on an ongoing basis, working on our "template of excellence" which is made up of comprehensive and structured systems and processes. This will be important when we roll out our franchising capability later this year.

Economic Advantage: This is another important factor in our success. We are pretty fanatical when it comes to pricing and margins and we try to avoid the word discount like the plague. We invest significantly in marketing especially in looking after our members and generating referrals. We have also invested in the best locations in our markets in our 3 new stores in Charlotte, Raleigh and Wilmington.

Phenomenon™ Experience

I am not sure if we deserve "Phenomenon™" status yet but the performance of our Charlotte store certainly deserves mention. The store opened for business in May 2007 and progressed in 2008 as follows:

- Sales from $0.5m in 2007 to $1.25m in 2008
- Herd from 2500 at end of 2007 to 7000 at end of 2008
- Referrals averaging 100 a month

Within a year of opening Charlotte came 1st in the South Atlantic Region and 2nd in the Nation in the Runners World specialty running store awards. By the way, our Mount Pleasant store came 2nd in the Region and 3rd in the Nation, a result that did not overly please them!

But the Phenomenon™ Experience of TrySports is best summed up with the following testimonial:

Testimonial from Sandra Szoke

I wanted to thank you from the bottom of my heart. I can't tell you how wonderful it was to watch my 67 year old dad at TrySports. I don't have a memory of him ever being that excited – no kidding. He is a low key kinda dad, but he has called me 4-5 times since he got his new bike, just to gush over it. He loves it, he loves his new pants, he loves his new computer, pedals – all of it.

Most of all, he really enjoyed the way that you guys paid attention to every little detail for him. He felt like he was the most important customer you ever had in the store. I didn't want to tell him that you treat everyone that way. It was an experience for him and he is telling everyone about it. Please pass my thanks to everyone.

Don't take what you do lightly. I have a dad who's happier than I can remember in a long, long time thanks to you guys!

Business Today

We have gone from 1 to 4 stores in a relatively short period of time. From 2007 to 2008 our sales have gone from $1.6 to $3.1 million. Our "herd" has grown from 11,000 to 20,000. And we have increased our annual referrals from 1500 to 2600.

In what is undoubtedly a very demanding economic environment, our Mount Pleasant store continues to do very well, while our Charlotte store continues its impressive growth and development. Our two new stores are making steady progress and the outlook for 2009 overall is good.

What's the future for TrySports? We are always developing. We are always looking to improve. We are still learning. We've lots to do. We plan to roll out our franchise capability later in 2009. For us really The Phenomenon™ has only started.

**To find out more about TrySports go to www.trysports.com.
If you are interested in learning more about a TrySports
franchise send an e-mail to jimkirwan@trysports.com.**

Phenomenon™ Practicioners by Industry

Authors/Getting Published/Publicity
Bill Harrison & Steve Harrison, Bradley Communications
www.freepublicity.com

Automotive Repair
Ron Ipach, CinRon Marketing
www.cinron.com

Chiropractic
Dr. Ben Altadonna
www.benaltadonna.com

College Planning
Ron Caruthers, College Planning Specialists, Inc.
www.collegeplanning.com

Commercial Real Estate Brokers
Jim Gillespie
www.realestatesalescoach.com

Dentistry
Dr. Charles Martin
www.martinsmiles.com

Ed O'Keefe
www.dentistprofits.com

eBay, Profiting from eBay
Andrew Lock, Andrew Lock Consulting
www.andrewlock.com

Internet Marketing
Derek Gehl, Internet Marketing Center
www.marketingtips.com

Ryan Lee
www.ryanlee.com

Yanik Silver, SureFire Marketing
www.surefiremarketing.com

Martial Arts
Lloyd Irvin, Emory Marketing Systems
www.lloydirvin.com

Mortgage Brokers
Michael Miget, Miget Marketing Systems
www.mortgagemarketingmaverick.com

Brian Sacks, Loan Officer Formula
www.loanofficerformula.com

Scott Tucker, Tucker Marketing Systems
www.mortgagemarketinggenius.com

Performance & Productivity
Lee Milteer
www.milteer.com

Real Estate
Ron LeGrand
www.ronlegrand.com

Rob Minton, Paramount Wealth Group
www.quitworksomeday.com

Sherman Ragland
www.shermanragland.com

Tim Winders
www.thefreedomequation.com

Retail
Bill Glazer, BGS Marketing
www.bgsmarketing.com

Trade Schools
Gene Kelly, ATI Trade Schools
www.atitradeschools.com

- TWO CDs Of The **EXCLUSIVE GOLD AUDIO INTERVIEWS**

These are EXCLUSIVE interviews with <u>successful users of direct response advertising, leading experts and entrepreneurs in direct marketing, and famous business authors and speakers</u>. Use them to turn commuting hours into **"POWER Thinking" Hours.**

★ **The New Member No B.S. Income Explosion Guide & CD** (Value = $29.97)
This resource is <u>especially designed for NEW MEMBERS</u> to show them HOW they can join the thousands of Established Members **creating exciting sales and PROFIT growth** in their Business, Practices, or Sales Careers & Greater SUCCESS in their Business lives.

★ **Income Explosion FAST START Tele-Seminar with Dan Kennedy, Bill Glazer, and Lee Milteer** (Value = $97.00)
Attend from the privacy and comfort of your home or office...hear a DYNAMIC discussion <u>of Key Advertising, Marketing, Promotion, Entrepreneurial & Phenomenon strategies</u>, PLUS answers to the most Frequently Asked Questions about these Strategies

★ **You'll also get these Exclusive "Members Only" Perks:**

- **Special FREE Gold Member CALL-IN TIMES.**
- **Gold Member RESTRICTED ACCESS WEBSITE.**
- **Continually Updated MILLION DOLLAR RESOURCE DIRECTORY**

*There is a one-time charge of $19.95 in North America or $39.95 International to cover postage for 2 Issues of the FREE Gold Membership. After your 2-Month FREE test-drive, you will automatically continue at the <u>lowest</u> Gold Member price of $49.97 per month ($59.97 outside North America). Should you decide to cancel your membership, you can do so at any time by calling Glazer-Kennedy Insider's Circle™ at 410-825-8600 or faxing a cancellation note to 410-825-3301 (Monday through Friday 9am – 5pm). Remember, your credit card will NOT be charged the low monthly membership fee until the beginning of the 3rd month, which means you will receive 2 full issues to read, test, and **profit from all of the powerful techniques and strategies you get from being an Insider's Circle Gold Member.** And of course, it's impossible for you to lose, because if you don't absolutely LOVE everything you get, you can simply cancel your membership after the second free issue and never get billed a single penny for membership.

EMAIL REQUIRED IN ORDER TO NOTIFY YOU ABOUT THE GLAZER-KENNEDY UNIVERSITY WEBINARS AND FAST START TELESEMINAR

Name _____ Business Name_____

Street Address _____

City _____ State _____ Zip _____ e-mail*_____

Phone _____ Fax_____

Credit Card Instructions to Cover $19.95 Postage ($39.95 International):

Credit Card: ____Visa ____MasterCard _____ American Express _____ Discover

Credit Card Number _____ Exp. Date _____

Signature _____ Date _____

Providing this information constitutes your permission for Glazer-Kennedy Insider's Circle to contact you regarding related information via mail, e-mail, fax, and phone.

ACT NOW!

www.In12MonthsGift.com
FAX BACK TO 410-825-3301
Or mail to: 401 Jefferson Ave., Towson, MD 21286

For Fastest Delivery Go Online Here!

The

PHENOMENON™

Achieve **More** in The **Next 12 Months** Than The **Previous 12 Years**

If you'd like to receive a **FREE** Video and if you're ready to experience The Phenomenon™ in <u>your</u> life – where you can **Achieve MORE in the Next 12 Months than in the Previous 12 Years** – PLUS have Dan Kennedy personally guide you through the *Step-by-Step Phenomenon™ System* then visit

http://www.In12MonthsCourse.com

Here's a Small Sample of What Dan will Cover:

- Foundations Required…a Deeper Understanding of The Phenomenon™
- **EIGHT Chief Phenomenon™ TRIGGERS**
- Marketing that Triggers The Phenomenon™
- **HOW to Break Out of "Slow" Prison**
- And Much MORE!!

For More Information and to Claim your FREE <u>Video</u>, Please Visit:

http://www.In12MonthsCourse.com

TreeNeutral

Advantage Media Group is proud to be a part of the Tree Neutral™ program. Tree Neutral offsets the number of trees consumed in the production and printing of this book by taking proactive steps such as planting trees in direct proportion to the number of trees used to print books. To learn more about Tree Neutral, please visit **www.treeneutral.com**. To learn more about Advantage Media Group's commitment to being a responsible steward of the environment, please visit **www.advantagefamily.com/green**

www.ingramcontent.com/pod-product-compliance
Lightning Source LLC
Jackson TN
JSHW011935131224
75386JS00041B/1398